★★★★★
BLACK POT

SUREFIRE METHODS
TO GET A
GREAT
DUTCH OVEN DISH
EVERY TIME

FOR

BEGINNERS

MARK'S BLACK POT

★★★★★★

BLACK POT

SUREFIRE METHODS
TO GET A
GREAT
DUTCH OVEN DISH
EVERY TIME

FOR

BEGINNERS

MARK HANSEN

HOBBLE CREEK PRESS
AN IMPRINT OF CEDAR FORT, INC.
SPRINGVILLE, UTAH

ISBN 13: 978-1-59955-974-2

Published by Hobble Creek Press, an imprint of Cedar Fort, Inc.
2373 W. 700 S., Springville, UT 84663
Distributed by Cedar Fort, Inc., www.cedarfort.com

LIBRARY OF CONGRESS CATALOGING-IN-PUBLICATION DATA

Hansen, Mark (Rulon Mark), author.
  Black pot for beginners : methods to get a great dutch oven dish every time / Mark Hansen.
    pages cm
  Includes bibliographical references and index.
  Summary: Step by step instructions for dutch oven beginners.
  ISBN 978-1-59955-974-2 (alk. paper)
  1. Dutch oven cooking. 2. Cooking, American. I. Title.

  TX840.D88.H37 2012
  641.5'89--dc23

                    2012021705

Cover design by Angela D. Olsen
Cover photography by Savannah Woods
Cover design © 2012 by Lyle Mortimer
Page design by Kelley Konzak
Edited and typeset by Casey Winters

Printed in the United States of America

10 9 8 7 6 5 4 3 2 1

Printed on acid-free paper

PRAISE FOR
BEST OF THE BLACK POT

"A fantastic book full of black pot magic. This book is a must-have for the Dutch oven enthusiast, whether beginner or pro."

—Matt Pelton, author of *The Cast Iron Chef* and
From Mountaintop to Tabletop and winner of the 2012
IDOS World Championship Dutch Oven Cook-off

"Mark Hansen makes Dutch oven cooking sound and feel like fun! Anyone picking up this book will be heading out to buy their first Dutch oven. It's very informative, with easy-to-follow recipes and a little history of each. I would recommend this cookbook to all beginners and also to the more 'seasoned' Dutch oven cooks."

—Omar Alvarez, winner of the 2008 IDOS
World Championship Dutch Oven Cook-off

"I'd call it 'Everything you ever wanted to know about Dutch oven cooking . . . and then some.' Dutch oven cooking can be intimidating to the beginner, but this book is full of easy-to-understand information. There is something for both the novice and seasoned black pot chef. This book is full of good recipes, fun stories, and insights on life. Reading it feels like a conversation with an old friend."

—Toni Black, dutchovenmadness.blogspot.com

"Mark has gone the extra mile and made this book self-explanatory. Beginners will be thrilled with the simple way he explains the cooking directions. Every cook starts somewhere, and this book comes highly recommended from me!"

—Colleen Sloan, author of the Log Cabin Grub series

"A fun, easy read. Though it is a fine cookbook covering much of what anyone needs to know about cooking with a Dutch oven, it provides many great recipes for the experienced cook. The book is also presented in a storytelling narrative—preparation, recipes, humor, and advice are presented entertainingly. This is a fun book that covers what you need to cook successfully in a Dutch oven."

—Stew Gaylord, Florida's IDOS Cracker Trail Chapter

CONTENTS

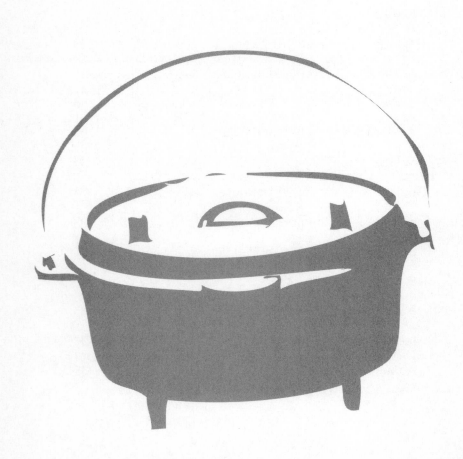

INTRODUCTION

UP THROUGH May 2006, I had no real interest in cooking.

I could make dinner in a pinch. I had a repertoire of about five dishes that I knew how to make, and they all tasted pretty good. On occasion, I had been known to bust out a recipe and make something a little fancier, but not often.

In May 2011, I was asked to write a cookbook.

Somewhere between 2006 and 2011, I learned how to cook. "Learned how to cook" is, of course, relative. I'm not sure that anyone thinks that they're done "learning how to cook," just like you're never done learning how to play the violin, how to fix a car, how to be a good parent, or anything else.

So somehow, in those few years, I went from apathetic and ignorant to enthusiastic to relatively confident and moderately competent.

It all started when my dear wife—remembering once that I had mentioned somewhere, somehow, somewhen, that I'd like to learn to cook in a Dutch oven—bought me one for Father's Day. I was excited. I don't know why. I know why I love Dutch oven cooking *now*, but I really don't know why it caught my attention back then.

I jumped right in and did some research. I decided my first attempt would be pizza, because I'd remembered doing that on a Scout camp many years before. I got some crust mix, some sauce, some toppings and cheese, and I was set. I read up on coals and seasoning the oven (which I attempted). One Sunday afternoon after church, I did my first Dutch oven dish, and it was delicious!

1

Many dishes and attempts to cook and bake all kinds of things then followed. Some were successful (like the potatoes, onions, and chicken in the first lesson), and others, well, not so much (like the apple pie that ended up like applesauce, or the many paperweights and doorstops that were supposed to be loaves of bread).

I bought many Dutch oven cookbooks and many regular cookbooks. I watched food shows on TV (I'll rant about that some other day). I tried many, many dishes. After almost a year, my friend John—of mormonfoodie.com fame—encouraged me to start a blog and share what I'd learned.

Here's the deal, though: I wasn't so much learning to cook in a Dutch oven as I was learning to cook, in a Dutch oven.

Let me state that carefully: I was learning how to cook. I also happened to be doing it in a Dutch oven.

See, cooking is really all about taking some food and putting heat to it. When you apply heat to food in just the right amounts and for the right length of time, magical things happen. Flavors change, textures shift, and tastes blend. Throughout the history of mankind, there have been many ways and styles of doing all of that. People have invented many devices and places and techniques to heat up food. They can bake it, roast it, fry it, sauté it, boil it, simmer it, braise it, brown it, broil it, steam it, smoke it, grill it, nuke it, or even just leave it out in the sun. For some reason, I had found that I loved to put it into a heavy cast-iron pot and put hot coals on top.

My real point is that in order to learn how to use a cast-iron pot, it's really much more about learning to cook. And learning how to do it using the Dutch oven. That's why I chose the title for the opening chapter as I did, and that's why I'm organizing the chapters the way I am. I hope to show that Dutch oven cooking is more than cobblers and counting coals. You truly can learn how to cook this way.

WHY I DUTCH OVEN

In the five years since I started doing this, I've learned why I love the Dutch oven so much and why it's my cooking method of choice.

IT'S SLOW

We live in a microwave and fast-food world. We grab breakfast as we dash out the door, we pick up dinner on our way home, and we throw things together at the last minute. We cook because we're hungry, and we do it fast because we need to check more things off our to-do lists.

I'm caught up in this as much as the next guy. I rush to work and shuffle my kids off to activities and appointments. My life is way too full, and my head spins as it plunges into my pillow in exhaustion at the end of the day.

Except on Sunday. Sunday, after church, is my cooking day. It's precious time to me. Life slows down. I can cook up something not only because we're all wanting to eat at dinnertime but also because it's going to be delicious. I can take the extra time to cook it slowly to make sure the flavors develop. I can breathe in the aromas deeply and savor the samples along the way. I can turn a few fresh ingredients into something amazing, I can take a few hours to do it . . . and I can sit and watch the coals burn down as dinner cooks. Don't bother me. I'm cooking.

IT'S EASY BUT CHALLENGING

Because, at its core, it's simply the process of heating up food, Dutch oven cooking is no different than cooking in other circumstances, like indoors.

However, it's also a bit more challenging: There are more variables when cooking this way. Regulating the temperature can be tricky, especially in varying weather conditions. Mother nature doesn't always cooperate. Cooking times can change. And ingredients respond differently.

Making a meal on your stove is something you do every day. Making it on your back porch or while camping in the wild is another thing altogether!

IT'S VERSATILE

Really, there are few meals that you can't cook in a Dutch oven. Part of my experimentation is driven toward finding those meals, and I haven't found anything so far. Some things have to be adapted a bit, but really, it's all fair game!

I get a special kick out of sharing something I've just cooked with someone and having them say incredulously, "You cooked *that* in a Dutch oven?"

IT'S DELICIOUS

Someone once told me that the worst dish in a Dutch oven is still better than most dishes from a regular stove. I don't know if I fully agree. I've cooked a few things (like the Great Corned Beef and Cabbage Disaster of 2007) that might change his mind. Still, Dutch oven cooking has a mystique to it, a magic that translates into flavor.

Part of this magic comes from the way the heavy lid traps the moisture, steaming the food. Another part, I'm sure, comes from the slow, even heat of the cast iron. Part of it even comes from the extra care I take when I'm cooking our Sunday dinners. Whatever the reason, the magic is there. The proof is in the flavor.

IT'S IMPRESSIVE

A long time ago, I made a really fancy dinner for my wife and some friends for Mother's Day. I did a crown roast of pork. I can still remember hefting the huge, 14-inch, deep Dutch oven onto the trivet on the table and lifting off the lid. The steam wafted up, and the smell hit them first. Then, when our vision cleared, that glazed, rich roast was there in the pot with the oranges and the veggies, and it looked *soooo goood*. I heard a collective gasp from everyone around. This was one of my finer culinary moments.

When you pull off something like that (or the family's Thanksgiving turkey or a special treat) and your friends are amazed that it came from your back porch instead of your stove, you feel joy! Even the easy stuff, at a campout or a backyard party, will thrill and delight.

IT'S SOCIAL

It's fun to cook for others, and it's also fun to cook *with* others. Organizations exist to promote the joys of Dutch oven cooking; we'll talk about these in more detail later on, but there's nothing like coming together with your gear and your ingredients to a "Dutch oven gathering," or DOG, and sharing your food and your fun. I don't experience this joy nearly as often as I would like.

IT'S TRADITIONAL AND HISTORICAL

Part of me, while I'm cooking on my back porch, thinks of my ancestors who crossed the dreary plains in covered wagons and handcarts, cooking their evening meals by the trailside in their own Dutch ovens. True, they probably didn't cook some of the crazy things I do, but I somehow connect with them when I'm cooking.

IT'S PRACTICAL

I know a lady (a fellow Dutch oven blogger: dutchovenmadness.com) who cooked for her family for a whole year in her Dutch ovens and blogged about it. Not long after completing her twelve-month cycle, their regular stove gave out. However, she was ready, and she was still able to feed her family.

I don't have a personal story quite that dramatic. But during the occasional stormy night, when the power has gone out, I've been able to cook for my family as well. It's fun to note that on those nights, we don't just eat, we eat well.

IT'S FUN

To me, this is really what it all comes down to. If I didn't enjoy learning new skills, trying new dishes, and making delicious food, I wouldn't still be doing it years later. I wouldn't be cooking. I wouldn't be blogging about it. And I definitely wouldn't be writing any cookbooks.

HOW TO SHOP FOR A DUTCH OVEN

If you're going to cook in a Dutch oven, of course you'll need to have one. This alone can be an intimidating proposition. Don't be overwhelmed by it. Really, you can cook in any Dutch oven. Read on, and you'll make a smarter first purchase.

Someone posted on my Facebook fan page a while back, asking a question I get asked often: "How do I shop for a Dutch oven? How do I know what to look for? How do I buy one that's the best for me?"

It depends on what you're looking for. That's the simple answer, but let's break it down. I'm presuming, by the way, that those reading this chapter are probably buying their first Dutch oven. If you've already got one or two and you're looking to buy another, you'll still be looking for the same basic things, but your reasons for buying will be different, and you'll possibly have a different result.

Consider four basic variables when deciding which Dutch oven to buy: the type, the size, the material, and the quality.

THE TYPE

You have two basic options for Dutch ovens: "camp" or "stove." Your best choice will depend on what type of cooking you'll be doing.

A camp Dutch oven is primarily designed for outdoor cooking using wood coals or charcoal briquettes. This oven type has a lip around the perimeter of the lid, which keeps the coals on the lid and prevents ash from falling down into the food when you lift it. It also has legs on the bottom that elevate the oven above any coals you want to put underneath.

A stove Dutch oven is designed primarily for indoor use. This oven type doesn't have legs, because you'll be setting it in your oven or resting it directly on your stove's burner, and it doesn't have the lip around the lid because you won't be setting coals on top. Some of these ovens will even be coated in colored enamels.

It *is* possible to use a camp Dutch oven indoors, but it's not as convenient. It's also possible to use a stove Dutch oven outdoors, but it's tricky.

THE SIZE

Dutch ovens are primarily measured by diameter and sometimes by quart capacity. Common sizes are 10- and 12-inch. You can buy them as small as 5 inches or as large as 22 inches (which take considerable effort to lift, even without food in them). Which one you end up buying will depend largely on who you'll be cooking for. If you're cooking for yourself or you have a small family, you won't want a big one. If you have a larger family or you're thinking you'll end up cooking for groups of friends, you'll want a bigger one. Dutch ovens can also be "shallow" or "deep." A 12-inch, shallow oven, for example, would be 12 inches in diameter, about 3½–4 inches deep, and have a capacity of about 6 quarts. A 12-inch, deep Dutch oven, on the other hand, would be about 5 inches deep and have a capacity of about 8 quarts.

If this is your first oven and you're merely interested in experimenting a little, I'd recommend a 12-inch, shallow oven. This will have the capacity to feed a family of four with some leftovers, and it can easily cook for a gathering of as many as eight, depending on what you're cooking. Breads, stews, chilis, desserts, and even small roasts can easily be done in a 12-inch Dutch oven.

Larger and smaller ovens will come in handy in more specialized situations. For example, I use my 14-inch, deep Dutch ovens to cook turkeys and larger specialty meats. I use my 8-inch oven for sides of rice or sauces.

THE MATERIAL

The two basic materials used to make Dutch ovens are cast iron and aluminum. Both have advantages and disadvantages. Even though all of my Dutch ovens are cast iron, I've seen chefs that swear by each material.

Cast iron is probably the most popular. It's the historic choice. It heats evenly (if slowly), and it holds the heat well, so your food stays warm in it, even after it's done cooking. It can take a lot of heat without damage too. Unfortunately, it's also quite heavy, and the bigger the oven, the heavier it is. Cast iron has to be seasoned to be used effectively, but with regular use, that seasoning patina gets better and better, and it becomes nonstick. Cast iron also lasts forever.

An aluminum Dutch oven is much lighter than cast iron, so it's often the pot of choice for campers, river runners, and backpackers who carry their gear in to their campsites. It won't rust, so you don't need to season it. It heats up quickly, but that also means that it cools quickly, and it's prone to developing hot spots.

Some say that cast iron–cooked food tastes better, but I've tasted delicious food from both kinds.

THE QUALITY

The best Dutch ovens I've ever seen come from three companies: Lodge, Camp Chef, and Maca. There are lots of littler brands, like Texsport and a few that are even no-name. Some Dutch oven chefs I know will swear by one brand or another. While it's true that some brands are better made, keep in mind that our pioneer ancestors cooked successfully in Dutch ovens made hundreds of years before modern companies were formed and contemporary casting procedures were invented. I've cooked delicious meals in off-brand Dutch ovens. I prefer my Lodge, but you can be successful with anything. You can even come across Dutch ovens at yard sales or antique stores.

Here are some tips for checking the quality:

First, check to see that the lid fits well. Press down on the lip of the lid all the way around. If you find a spot where the lid rocks back and forth, that's a sign of a poorly fitting lid. That will let more moisture escape when you're cooking. Again, you can still cook well in that pot, but it won't be quite as effective.

Some off-brands will use different alloys or different sources for their cast-iron stock. This can make for variations in the thickness of the pot and the density of the metal. In either case, this can cause uneven heating and hotspots. Unfortunately, you can't really check for that in the store. It's one reason you might want to go with a more respected brand. Still, my forefathers who crossed the plains didn't have a Lodge or a Camp Chef.

SEASONING

I should add a note or two about seasoning and how that impacts your purchase as well. The seasoning is the black coating of burned-on oils that gives the Dutch oven its characteristic blackness. It keeps the Dutch oven from rusting, helps transfer the heat to the food, and also builds up, over time, to be an amazing non-stick surface as good as Teflon!

Most of the major manufacturers (and many of the off-brands and no-names as well) now sell all of their Dutch ovens pre-seasoned. This makes it much more convenient for you, the beginner. That's one less step between you and your first successful dish.

You might, however, acquire an oven from an older stock, and it might need to be seasoned. If so, it will look silver instead of black. You might pick up an old Dutch oven at a yard sale or as a cast-off from a family member or friend. It might need to be reseasoned. If either of these is the case, you'll learn how to do it, since we'll talk about seasoning in lesson six.

SUMMING IT ALL UP

Okay, so this is really a seventy-five-dollar answer to a ten-dollar question. What Dutch oven should I buy? My recommendation is that if you want to get started in outdoor Dutch oven cooking, get a 12-inch, shallow Lodge or Camp Chef, pre-seasoned. You'll possibly notice that almost all of the recipes on my blog use that basic size. My two 12-inchers are the workhorses of my cast iron collection.

Whatever you end up buying, you now have some knowledge to help you make a wise choice, either to get started or to expand once you've gotten a few recipes down!

HOW TO USE THIS BOOK

A lot of the Dutch oven books I've seen have a few words about Dutch ovening, with some tips and general rules about coal counting or what gear to have, and then a lot of recipes. That's great, but that's not the approach I want to take. I want to spell it out for you, step by step, so you'll feel all the success and none of the fear. It's true that we learn by trial and error, but I've found that this leads to mostly error. With a bit of detailed guidance, you can reduce the error, resulting in a faster process.

So with that in mind, I've separated the book into nine lessons. Each one will teach a concept that I feel is essential to learning how to cook, in a Dutch oven, including Dutch oven things, like coals and heat management, and more cooking-related things, like knife skills and baking. Each lesson will introduce the concept and then show you a dish or two that you can cook to practice that concept.

Feel free to skip around, if you like, but if you take the lessons one at a time, you'll grow in confidence and skill. And then you'll be able to go after recipes in all kinds of Dutch oven cookbooks as well as indoor cookbooks. You'll soon be creating your own culinary works of art.

Your family and friends will get excited to try your next effort, and you'll thrill them with your dishes and delicacies.

You'll be a Dutch oven chef!

THE LESSONS

LESSON 1: INSTANT SUCCESS
The purpose of the first lesson is to get you started with a delicious and easy one-pot meal of chicken and potatoes. It's simple to prepare and cook, but it looks and tastes much fancier. It also has plenty of room for improvisation. Most important: It's really, really hard to mess it up!

I'll introduce you to a few essential Dutch oven cooking tools and the real basics of heat management. You'll also learn how to properly clean up and store your Dutch ovens. After this, however, you might like it so much that you won't want to store it for long!

LESSON 2: THE DUTCH OVEN AND THE GEAR
Once you've had your first taste of success (pun intended), you'll learn more about the Dutch oven itself. We'll learn a bit about its history and origins, and we'll learn about how to get it (and keep it) looking black and shiny! We'll talk about some other bits of Dutch oven gear you'll want to shop for, and I'll guide you in getting the right stuff.

The lesson two dish is a traditional dump cake cobbler. This is another simple dish that wows people every time. It's almost embarrassingly easy to do.

LESSON 3: BASIC CHEFFERY
In this lesson, you're going to learn some cooking basics. You'll learn what things

you'll need in order to have a well-equipped outdoor kitchen. I'll talk about the second most important purchase you'll make, after the Dutch ovens themselves: the chef's knife. This is as important to the chef as a rifle is to a hunter.

Once you have a good yet inexpensive chef's knife, you'll learn how to wield it to chop, slice, dice, and mince the veggies and meat that go into a great chili or stew. You'll learn how to use your Dutch oven to sauté, brown, boil, and simmer.

LESSON 4: MORE SOUPS, STEWS, AND CUTS
With all of those good basic skills, you'll want to practice them and expand on them a bit. In this lesson, I'll show you how to do a few more cuts and a few more impressive soups and stews.

LESSON 5: HEAT AND MEAT
In lesson five, you'll slow roast some beef or ham, and in the process you'll learn about heat and heat management. You'll learn how to rotate coals through longer, slower cooking times that make meats come out tender and juicy. This process takes more time, but it will all pay off when you lift that lid and the rich, savory aroma swirls around you and your family or friends!

LESSON 6: HERBS, SPICES, AND FLAVORINGS
Since the early history of Western civilization, herbs and spices have driven politics, conquest, and exploration. In this lesson, you'll learn how to master them and make them work for you! You'll learn how to make your own favorite spice and herb blends. Since you'll already know how to manage long cook times, you'll be able to try them out on a succulent roast chicken or turkey!

LESSON 7: FLOUR, SODA, AND HEAT, PART 1
With all of the savory meats at your command now, I'll turn your attention to the most common accompaniment: quick breads. I'll talk about how baking sodas and baking powders make biscuits and soda breads fluffy and light. I'll also talk about how to regulate the heat with more precision to make the baking more effective. And I'll talk, of course, about how *not* to burn the bottoms!

LESSON 8: FLOUR, SODA, AND HEAT, PART 2
Finally, we get to have dessert! This lesson explores how to make sweets using your Dutch ovens and the same chemical leavens discussed previously. You can make beautiful and delicious cakes, brownies, and cookie bars to bring some sugar to the end of a savory meal.

LESSON 9: PUTTING IT ALL TOGETHER
You've learned how to do long, slow roasts and deep, rich stews. You can make

biscuits that would make your gramma raise her eyebrows. You can even bake a birthday cake! At this point, you might have actually considered acquiring other Dutch ovens and bits of cast-iron cookery. I'll teach you a bit about the different sizes, how to judge them, and what on earth to use them for! Then I'll show you how to plan out a whole meal, from choosing the recipes to creating the shopping lists and planning out the cooking timeline.

And now that you know how to cook in a Dutch oven, you'll want to share it around! Invite over family and friends. Join a Dutch oven society. Go to a Dutch oven gathering or even do a cook-off! Many other people out there share your interest, either in cooking in the Dutch oven or just eating what comes out of it!

APPENDIX: MORE RECIPES
Finally, we'll wrap the book up with some more good recipes.

So . . .

Shall we get started?

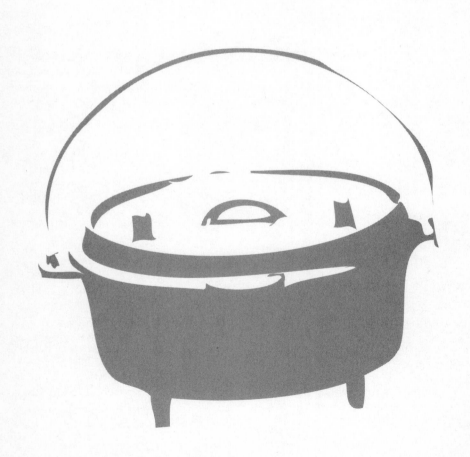

INSTANT SUCCESS

CHICKEN AND POTATOES

SO, BY now you should have acquired a Dutch oven. I'm going to assume, for simplicity's sake, that you have a seasoned, 12-inch, shallow Dutch oven. If you don't, you can either go get one, or you can adapt what I'll be teaching you to whatever size and shape of Dutch oven you do have. It's not that tough to do.

The whole purpose of this chapter is to let you cook something and have that great feeling of success. While there's no such thing as a foolproof, error-proof, guaranteed hit in cooking, if you follow these directions, it's not likely that you'll go wrong. In a total of about two hours of prep and cooking time, you'll have a delicious, one-pot meal that you can serve to a family or group of four to six people.

Before we start cooking, however, you'll need to acquire a few tools and supplies, and you'll also want to shop for the ingredients.

THE LID LIFTER
The whole point of this effort will be to get the Dutch oven really hot to cook the food. So you'll want to have some ways to handle the Dutch oven without actually handling it. The best tool in your kit for this will be some kind of lid lifter.

Companies all over make commercial lid lifters, and they basically come down to two types: the hook-style and the Mair-style.

The hook is the most common and the simplest. It's just a metal bar bent into a hook. Some of these also include a T-shaped crossbar welded on. This helps to stabilize the lid as you're lifting it so that you don't tip coal ash into your food. Some people refer to this as "campfire pepper" and get along with it. I prefer to minimize it as much as possible; I like the taste of real pepper much better.

In recent years, a brand named Mair has come along with a really great design for a lid lifter. It hooks under the lid loop, like the hook-style, but it uses a clamp-like motion with three legs that grip the lid tight. This makes it even more stable and even less likely to shake the ash in. You can lift the lid without tipping it.

Now, I've used both of these, and I think they both work well. You can buy either one in a variety of lengths. Using the longer ones means that you don't have to bend down as far to get the lid off, and using the shortest ones means that your hands are a lot closer to the heat of the coals. I think the midrange lengths are the most useful, overall. Speaking for myself, I prefer the stability of the Mair-style lifters.

However, I've also seen people, in the absence of anything fancy, use a pair of pliers or vice-grips or even a hammer hook. It's amazing what you can use if you're clever and resourceful. You don't have to spend a lot of money.

When the dinner is all cooked and done, any of these options can also be used with the wire bail (handle) on a Dutch oven to lift and carry the oven to the hungry masses you're wanting to feed. The wire bails rest close to the coals and get very hot.

CHARCOAL TONGS

You'll be shifting red-hot glowing coals from your burning stack and putting them under and on top of your Dutch oven. I know this may surprise you, but I don't recommend doing that with your bare hands—something about avoiding the local hospital's burn ward, and the insurance issues . . .

Get some longer food tongs (about a foot and a half, at least), with some kind of spring-opening action. This will allow you to grab as many as two or three burning coals at a time and move them to exactly where you want them. Once they're on the Dutch oven or the cooking surface, you can push them around with the tongs as well, for exact placement. I like tongs a bit longer because they keeps my hands far away from the radiant heat of a stack of burning coals, which can get more intense than you might think.

Important Note: Once you begin using a set of tongs for moving coals, *do not* use it to move, stir, or handle food in any way. The tongs will get gunky and coated with lots of the burned and unburned chemicals that the charcoal briquettes carry. Have another separate set if you're going to be touching food. By the way, I like the shorter-handled ones for moving food.

CHARCOAL

Charcoal is the core of Dutch oven cooking because it's the fundamental heat source. Some people will use wood from a campfire to cook their Dutch oven meals. While people have been doing that for centuries and were able to cook meals that helped them live another day, it can be more difficult for a beginner to regulate the heat that way. For that reason, I recommend cooking with charcoal briquettes. It really is a more common practice in the modern Dutch oven world.

Which should you buy? Well, I've tried many different brands and some different styles. I think it's most important to be consistent. Anything that burns will give you heat. But different brands and types will burn differently. They'll have a unique "burning curve." Yes, I made that up.

Some coals will light quickly, burn fast, and then fade and go out. Others will light, take a while to fully catch, then suddenly get very hot. I like it when coals burn more steadily; they light and may even take a few more minutes to get white, but then they will burn long and steady before gradually dying out.

The following images are a sort of abstract representation of some of these charcoal burning curves, comparing time (x) to heat (y):

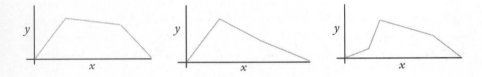

You can use any brand and type of charcoal as long as you're used to and expecting the kind of burning curve it will deliver. You'll know how long they will burn, when you'll have to replenish, and when they're going to be burning at their hottest. The last thing you want, especially in the middle of a tricky dish, is to have your coals go out or unexpectedly hit their heat peak.

Here are a few other things that I don't use: **Instant-light charcoal** has already been steeped in an accelerant, so you don't need to use any lighter fluid or paper. These tend to have a pretty hot and fast burning curve, and they need replenishing more frequently. I've seen meals almost ruined because the coals gave out before the dish was cooked with these. If you know what kind of curve you're up against, however, you can plan for it and make it work.

On the other hand, I've seen people add a few instant-light briquettes to the stack when lighting their fires, which helps to start regular briquettes faster, especially if they're on the bottom of the stack.

I also don't use **hickory** or **mesquite** or any **briquettes that are intermingled with any of the "flavor" woods**. These may be great for grilling or smoking, but when you put them under or on top of a Dutch oven, the flavored smoke won't get through the cast iron to the food anyway.

My brand of choice is good, reliable, steady-burning, normal Kingsford. You can use what you like.

And while we're at it, I'm going to go on record saying that I use lighter fluid. I'm sorry to any of the purists or environmentalists out there. Wadded up paper has never worked for me. It just doesn't burn long enough to light the briquettes. I have heard that if you drizzle some kind of cooking oil on the paper, it will burn longer. I haven't noticed a significant enough difference, honestly. I just squirt on a hefty amount of lighter fluid and fire it up. It doesn't explode like gasoline, but in moments, a good, hot fire is raging, starting up the coals.

Again, because the briquettes and their fumes don't get through the cast iron to the food, I'm not as concerned with any of the chemicals in the briquettes or the lighter fluid.

COOKING SPACE

The last thing to consider is where you're going to cook. By that, I mean two things: First, where within your space (like your yard, your patio, your campground, and so on) would you like your cooking area to be? Second, what actual surface will you be using for the coals and the Dutch ovens?

When I'm cooking our Sunday meals, I'm cooking on our back porch. There's a small concrete pad, and it has easy access to the back door. I usually prep the food in our kitchen and then move it to the cooking area outside, especially in the cold winter months.

When I first began Dutch ovening, I had heard that hot coals are bad for concrete. It turns out that this is only partially true. A big stack of coals can get very, very hot at the core. Since concrete doesn't conduct heat very well, the surface of the concrete where the coals are resting can get very hot and expand significantly. Under the surface, the remaining concrete doesn't transfer the heat as well, so it doesn't expand as much. As a result, the surface can crack, chip, and flake away.

As it turns out, occasionally cooking with a ring of coals that aren't packed too tightly together (which will be the case for most of your dishes) isn't going to hurt your concrete much.

Still, back in the day, I put a couple of 12 × 24 × 2 concrete pavers side by side and used that for my cooking surface. I made one set for the pot and one for the pile of burning coals. I guess I figured that even though the pavers were concrete, if they chipped and broke, it wouldn't be as bad as damaging the poured concrete pad.

Later on, I purchased a few small metal tables. Not only do they maintain the heat well but they also lift the Dutch ovens up just a little bit higher, so I'm not cooking quite so low to the ground. Some metal tables made just for Dutch oven cooking are commercially available. My dear, sweet wife recently bought me one, and I use it a lot now.

For your first dish, don't go out and spend a lot of money on fancier tools and tables. Spend a little time cooking and see what you like and how it works for you. Then you can get the right kind of accessories.

Frankly, if you've got a spot of hard-packed dirt, with no grass, then that's fine to cook on. I wouldn't use a spot where the dirt is soft because the weight of the Dutch oven and the food can make the small feet sink into the earth. Then the coals would be very close to the bottom of the Dutch oven and it could cause hot spots and uneven cooking.

Can you use a regular charcoal grill? Well, that depends. A typical grill has a space down below where you put the coals, and then the grid where you put the food. Usually, there's too much distance between the two. To put the coals below and the Dutch oven on the grid would probably put the food too far from the heat source, so you'd need to put more coals below. That would throw off the recipe instructions to get the right amount of heat. The legs on a Dutch oven are there to support the oven above the coals at an optimal distance: close enough to get good heat, far enough away for more even heating.

Can you cook in your garage? That depends on how well ventilated it is. Sometimes, in bad weather, I've done that. My garage, however, has the large opening for the cars at one end, and a side, walk-through door at the other end. With both of those doors wide open, the breeze can blow through and sweep away the carbon monoxide being put out by the coals. Carbon monoxide is created when burning is incomplete, when things are smoldering. Charcoals smolder rather than burn. If that gas is trapped in your garage, it can kill you. It can also get into your house and kill your family. Not a good before-dinner plan, if you ask me.

I much prefer to cook in open spaces, where there is plenty of fresh air swirling around me. Then carbon monoxide is not an issue.

The simple answer? Get yourself a couple of pavers or put a small square of solid gauge sheet metal on some bricks in the open air of your backyard, and you'll be good to go. Remember to have one space for your Dutch oven and one to light up the coals.

GETTING GOING
So your checklist for things to have so far should be:

- A 12-inch, shallow Dutch oven (or whatever you've got that's close to that)

- Something you can use to lift the lid and the Dutch oven

- A pair of long-handled tongs for the coals

- A bag or two of charcoal and something to light it

- Pavers (paving bricks) or some other surface to cook on

With that, we're ready to shop for ingredients! Read through the list on the next page and make out your shopping list. I can't count how many times I've started a dish, only to find out halfway through, in the middle of a critical cooking process, that I'm out of a key ingredient. Then I have to suddenly decide: (1) just how "key" it might be and (2) if I could run to the store in time to get it. Sometimes I'll ask a neighbor, but they don't always have what I need. Plus, doing that too much can get old for them, I'll bet.

DUTCH OVEN CHICKEN AND POTATOES

INGREDIENTS

3–4 boneless chicken breasts, fully thawed, drained, patted dry, and cubed

about ½ lb. bacon, precooked crispy (You can buy it this way at the store or do it yourself on the stove. You could do it in the Dutch oven, but that would complicate things
a bit, and we want to keep this first dish really simple.)

2–3 medium to large onions, sliced or diced

3–4 potatoes, quartered and sliced

2–3 carrots, sliced

3–4 celery stalks, sliced

2–3 sweet peppers, sliced or diced

1 heaping Tbsp. minced garlic

a few Tbsp. olive oil

liberal shakes of:

parsley

rosemary

oregano

a few shakes (about 1 tsp. or so) balsamic vinegar

and, of course, salt and pepper

PREPARING

Before any cooking begins, the food has to be prepared. And, in this case, it might
require some pre-preparation. Let's talk about the chicken and the bacon. If you
use frozen chicken breasts, make sure that they're well thawed and drained of
excess juices before you begin preparing the food. After you drain them, pat them
dry with paper towels or clean dish towels. The bacon should already be cooked
crispy and broken up into bits.

Once you've cubed up the chicken, clean the knife and the cutting board before
you begin working on the veggies to avoid any cross-contamination. You could
even use separate cutting surfaces. Germs from meats can wreak havoc in veggies
and germs in veggies can affect the meat.

In the proper culinary world, chefs talk of a concept called *mise en place* (pro-
nounced "meez-on-plahz," more or less). Literally translated it means to "put in
place." The idea is to get everything ready around you that you will need. I don't
always do this, myself; however, I should. I find that the times that I fully prepare,
things go much smoother than when I don't.

So, out in your cooking area, you'll gather your charcoal, tongs, and lid lifter—you'll
prepare your cooking surface. In your food prep area, you'll gather your ingredients,
cutting space and knife, and the Dutch oven.

LIGHTING THE COALS

Start by counting out between 35 and 40 coals. Look at about how big that stack of coals is. In the future, you'll get to the point where you won't need to count. The number above is an estimate anyway. We probably won't need that much, but it will be nice to have extra if we do. I have ruined many a meal by poor management of the coals. It's better to waste a few coals than to waste the food.

Douse the coals with some lighter fluid and fire them up. I like to start them in a pretty tight pile, rather than spread out. I think they light each other better that way.

PREHEATING AND SEASONING

Once the coals are lit and starting to get a bit of white on the edges, the next thing we're going to do is preheat and season the Dutch oven. Spread out 18–20 coals onto your cooking surface. Use spray oil to coat the surface of the Dutch oven and the lid. Concentrate on the interior, but get the exterior as well. Then set the Dutch oven above the coals. Set about the same amount of coals on the lid and put it on the Dutch oven. I usually don't set the lid exactly in place for the preheat/seasoning phase; rather, I set it a little to the side so there's a gap and so any smoke that comes from the oil can escape.

Here's the whole idea of this step: Not only does it get the Dutch oven ready for cooking, but it also sears another layer of oil in place in the patina. The more you do this, the better your oven's seasoning coating will be, and over the years it will turn into the best nonstick cookware you own.

Then go to your food prep area and get a couple of small to medium mixing bowls. In one, add in the chicken that you had cubed before and the bacon that you had either purchased or precooked.

Then start cutting up the veggies and put them into another bowl. We're not going to be picky at this point how they get cut or how you use the knife. We'll talk about all that in another chapter. For now, this is all about simplicity.

COOKING

Now we're ready to cook. It's time to make the food happen!

Take the meat and veggies out to the cooking space and pour 1–2 tablespoons of olive oil in the Dutch oven. Wait a few minutes while it heats up. If the oven is already hot, it won't take long. Take the Dutch oven off the coals. In the cooking area, make a ring of 10–12 coals. Put the others back in your charcoal pile. Set the Dutch oven in the center of the coals and tuck the coals under the edge of the oven. The heat will continue to radiate up the sides and inward to the center.

Add all the food you prepared earlier to the Dutch oven. Later on, as you learn about browning and sautéing and other things, you'll learn how to do things in proper order. For this first dish, however, you'll want to keep it simple, so dump in all the ingredients. The food will still taste great. Put the lid on the Dutch oven, fully seated in place. Use the tongs to arrange 16–18 coals in a circle around the rim of the lid. (Use more coals if it's cold or windy outside.) Put the rest in your charcoal pile. Just like the coals below, the heat will radiate toward the center of the lid. You need more coals on the lid because much of the heat will just rise up into the air.

Hold your hand about a foot above the coals and feel the heat. Make a mental note of what that feels like. Do this every time you set up some coals on your Dutch ovens, and soon you'll be able to tell if the coals are hot enough by feel.

Lift the lid and sprinkle in the seasonings. Don't be shy with the flavors. It is possible to use too much, but most times I see people using way too little. You'll be able to taste and add more as it's cooking. Stir it all up and reseat the lid.

Toss a half dozen or so fresh coals onto your pile of charcoal. These will start to catch, and you can use them if the ones on your Dutch oven need replenishing.

Now you can relax and watch. Sip a soda. Read a book.

After about 15 minutes, check the heat again. Tap the coals lightly with the tongs to knock off the ash. Lift the Dutch oven with your lid lifter and tap the bottom coals too. When you put the oven back on the coals, put it back a quarter turn or so from where it was. Turn the lid also: this will change the position of the coals relative to the food and will prevent hot spots and burning, which is not so important with this dish, but when you're doing breads, it will be critical. It's a good habit to get into anyway.

Use your lifter and check the food. Give it a stir to keep the food on the bottom from burning. It should be warm, even a bit hot, and it probably will be getting a bit done. It most likely won't be done yet, though. Don't spend a long time at this; just a quick lift and a stir. The less you lift the lid, the better.

Then go back to your soda and book. I can recommend a couple of good Dutch oven books, by the way . . .

In another 15 minutes, check it again and do the same process. This time when you stir, taste a few pieces and adjust the seasonings. Add what you want. Pay particular attention to the potatoes and the chicken because those will be the "doneness" indicators. When the potatoes are soft and the chicken is cooked all the way through, it's ready. At this point, it might be done or it might require an additional 10-minute cycle. If it does need to go longer, add a few coals from the pile onto the ring below and the lid above (in about the same ratio that was used in the start). Remember to replace the Dutch oven and the lid in a different rotation.

There may be some liquid in the Dutch oven, which has come from the veggies and the chicken. If there is a lot, you can thicken it into a sort of sauce. Take about ¼ cup of warm water and stir in about 1 tablespoon of flour or cornstarch. Stir it up briskly until it's runny and has no clumps.

Then stir a couple of tablespoons of the mixture into the Dutch oven and watch. If it gets thicker over a minute or two, then you're fine. Replace the lid and cook some more. If not, add another couple of tablespoons and stir that in. That should be enough.

In the last cooking cycle, it's a good time to have someone prep the serving/dining area. Get out some plates or bowls, silverware, cups, and so on.

Finally, after the last cooking cycle, the food should be done! Take the Dutch oven off the coals and set it a good distance away. Remove the lid and shake the remaining coals off over the charcoal pile. If there's even a light breeze, some of the ash dust will drift. This is why you set the food away from the cooking area. Ash drifting into the food is not good eats. Once the coals and ash are off the lid, you can put it back on the Dutch oven and bring it all to the serving/dining area. The cast iron will help keep the food warm for a long time.

At this point, gather everyone together and serve it up! You can dish it up directly from the Dutch oven. Since it already has meat and veggies, you can add a little bread on the side, and you're good to go.

You've just cooked your first Dutch oven dish! Isn't that exciting? How did it go?

CLEANUP

After everyone is done complimenting you on the absolutely delicious dish you made, it will be time for cleanup. Since you cooked the meal, you have every right to tell everyone else to clean the serving dishes. Even still, you'll want to learn how to clean the Dutch oven. It seems that there are as many different methods of cleaning Dutch ovens as there are chefs.

It's important to clean right away after eating so the food doesn't dry in place. If your Dutch oven is well seasoned, the food should be easy to clean away. Since I'm usually cooking on my back porch, I can clean my ovens in the sink. I just get the water as hot as possible and spray it out with my sink sprayer. Any stubborn chunks can be removed with a plastic-bristled brush. Don't use metal scratchers or scouring pads, as they can take off the patina.

Here's another big debate: detergent or not. I've heard experienced Dutch oveners argue on both sides. Some say that it will take off the patina; others say that mild detergents are fine. Honestly, with a good black coating, I've never found that I needed detergents. The food comes off pretty easily; even cheese and syrups come clean with a little scrubbing.

Whether or not you use detergent, nearly everyone agrees: do not use your dishwasher to clean your Dutch ovens.

Remember to scrub and rinse the ash off the lid and the bottom of the Dutch oven as well.

Once the oven has been cleaned, wipe it out with a paper towel and let it air-dry for a few minutes. It should be warm from the cooking and the hot water, so it shouldn't take long to dry. At that point, the oven is ready for storage. Some will say that you should coat the oven with a thin layer of oil at that point. I used to do that; it was fine for the Dutch ovens that I used week to week, but the ones I didn't use as much would sometimes get a nasty smell after a while because the oil would go rancid.

If the eating is happening away from home, a couple of options exist for cleaning. The obvious one is to pack the ovens away in the car and clean them when you get home. That's what I usually do. Of course, that assumes that I'm going home the same day.

If you're camping or not going home soon after, you'll have to clean it right there. Scrape out as much food as you can with a plastic scraper or wooden spoon. Put some water in the bottom of the Dutch oven and put it back on the remainder of the coals. After it has heated up, use a plastic brush to scrub off any loose bits. Use the water and the brush to rinse off the lid, then dispose of the water. Again, wipe the Dutch oven out with a paper towel and let it air-dry.

STORAGE

At this point, the Dutch oven is done, and it doesn't really matter much where you store it. Keep it where it will be dry, of course, and where it won't fall or drop. It can survive the temperature extremes of weather, so a carport or garage is fine. You can keep it in a box, a bag, or out in the open.

I recommend keeping it accessible because if it's packed away, buried underneath your tents and sleeping bags in your shed, you likely won't use it very often. I keep mine nicely stacked in a corner of my living room, by the door that leads to the back porch. Easy-access, rustic decor. It all works out.

Congratulations! You've just cooked, served, and cleaned up after your first Dutch oven meal! That's quite an accomplishment. Take a minute to feel good about that.

This is a really simple dish to cook successfully. As you continue through the book, you'll learn more and more ways to make this meal, and other things you cook, even better. The recipe above is good for a sort of herbal flavor. However, here are a few variations:

CHEESES

In the last cooking cycle, layer some grated cheese on top and let that melt. You could add a few coals to the lid and it might even brown a little. With chicken, I usually prefer a mild white cheese, like mozzarella or provolone, but why not something sharper like cheddar or Colby?

SOME LIKE IT HOT

Instead of the seasonings in the recipe above, try these for a spicy southwestern flavor:

1 heaping Tbsp. minced garlic
1–2 jalapeño peppers, sliced. If you don't like it really hot, you can seed and core them first, or use fewer
a few shakes of cayenne pepper, chili powder, or Louisiana-style hot sauce (Tabasco)
a few shakes of paprika
about ½ cup fresh, chopped cilantro
juice of 1–2 limes
and, of course, salt and pepper

or just pour in your favorite salsa

SPRINGTIME LEMON

This version really brightens up the flavors and makes it into a wholly different dish. If you use cheese on this one, instead of melting on mozzarella, wait until you serve it and grate some Parmesan or, even better, mizithra on it and crumble some feta on top! Mmmmm! A Mediterranean feast!

1 heaping Tbsp. minced garlic
½ cup fresh, chopped Italian parsley
zest of 1 lemon
juice of 1–2 lemons
and, of course, salt and pepper

Don't be afraid to add your own variations into it. Wonderful food can be fancy *and* simple!

REVIEW

Now, take a minute to analyze and see what you've learned.

You learned

- how to buy a Dutch oven;
- how to set up the heat;
- how to prepare all the basic ingredients;
- how to maintain stable heat throughout the cooking;
- how to handle the hot Dutch oven and lid;
- how to clean up the Dutch oven afterward; and
- how to store the Dutch oven.

ANALYSIS QUESTIONS

How did the chicken taste?

How were the seasonings?

Were the potatoes done to your liking?

What would you do differently next time?

LESSON 2

THE DUTCH OVEN AND THE GEAR

THE DUMP CAKE COBBLER

SO, NOW you've had your first taste of successful cooking in the Dutch oven. Woot! Way to go! Do a dance! But don't spike your Dutch oven like you just scored a touchdown.

Lesson two is all about the Dutch oven itself: where it came from, where it's going, and what you can do with it. We'll also get really practical, learning how to get and maintain the fine black coating, called the patina. Then, we'll talk a little more about the gear and accessories that you can use with your Dutch ovens; you can really spend a lot of money. We'll talk about why you should or shouldn't.

ALL ABOUT THE DUTCH OVEN
One quick Google search for the term "Dutch oven" will show you that there are a lot of very different meanings for the word. Two, in particular, stand out.

One of those is a cooking pot with some kind of lid that will trap the hot air and moisture of food when it cooks. The other is the practice of farting under heavy blankets, trapping the noxious fumes to be released when your spouse gets into bed.

Guess which one this book is about.

Even as we talk about the cooking pots, there are many, many variations of items referred to as "Dutch ovens." There are thin aluminum pots, which I would call "stockpots," and the deep, heavy, enameled pots that can be used on top of a range or in a conventional oven. I call these "roasting pots." There are also the cast-iron pots with no legs, intended for indoor use. Finally, we have the camp Dutch oven, which is what this book is about.

I'm not going to begrudge anyone their terminology. Let them name the Dutch oven how they may. I just know that when I think of my "Dutch ovens," I know what I'm talking about: it's cast iron, it's black, and it has legs and a rim on the lid!

THE HISTORY OF THE DUTCH OVEN

The history of the black pot is no less varied. Much of what has been written about its history is apocryphal, or at least legendary. By that I mean that many writers quote and cite each other as they go through the timeline. I'm not going to be any different. The important thing is not so much the dates but to get an overall picture of the Dutch oven's place in history and to feel some connection to that as you cook.

Well, really, when you think about it, you could cook just fine in a Dutch oven and never know that it existed before a month ago, right? But the more you learn about its background and its life, the more it makes sense. I find myself reading something and saying, "Oh! *That's* why they did it that way!"

PREHISTORY

After the Stone Age, people started hammering copper into shapes; then they discovered that copper could be blended with tin, resulting in the Bronze Age. Pretty soon, people were heating and hammering iron out of the rocks, and in the eleventh century BC, they learned how to make things with wrought iron and crude steels.

Then in 513 BC, the Chinese discovered how to make a furnace hot enough to actually melt the iron down, and casting iron began. Clever of those guys. The Europeans didn't figure out the blast furnace until about the twelfth century *after* Christ. They may be slow, but they get there.

Cast-iron pots and cauldrons were used to cook after that and were even mentioned in Shakespeare's plays (like being used by the witches in *Macbeth*).

LATE 1600s

By this time, the Dutch had a pretty sweet system of making molds out of sand, and they were putting out some good pots, pans, and other cast-iron things. These were, of course, being exported all over, particularly in England. This is one of the theories behind why they are called "Dutch ovens" today.

Another theory is that Dutch traveling traders spread the pots far and wide, so people referred to them as "Dutch ovens." Yet another theory about the name comes from the fact that the ovens had also been brought over with Dutch immigrants who had settled in Pennsylvania.

1700s

In 1704, an Englishman went to the Netherlands to study Dutch casting techniques. He brought those skills back to England, worked on them some more, and eventually received an English patent. He began producing his cookware and distributing it in England and the colonies in America. In Ireland, as well as in other places, the pots were made with small points hanging from the underside of the lid. As meats roasted, the steam would gather and drip down these points, giving the pot the name "bastible."

In America, the practicality and versatility of these ovens caught on quickly. They were perfect for hearth cooking, which is where almost all "cheffery" happened in homes. The ovens could roast meats, boil soups, and bake breads and cakes.

Adjustments and improvements came in America too, including the legs and lip around the lid to keep the ashes out of the food. Paul Revere is credited with coming up with the idea for the lip, but I have never seen any real evidence of that fact. It makes a good story, though.

In these days, cast-iron cookware was considered very valuable and, since it was also very durable, would be passed down from generation to generation. George Washington's mother, Mary Ball Washington, specified in her will how her "iron kitchen furniture" would be divided after her death.

1800s

In the early 1800s, the United States was growing, and soon the Dutch oven truly became an American icon. Lewis and Clark took Dutch ovens on their famous expedition to explore the Louisiana Purchase and find a route to the West Coast.

As explorers and pioneers moved west—including the Mormon migration—Dutch ovens crossed the plains with them. Several of these dauntless souls on my mother's side pushed handcarts all the way from Winter Quarters, on the east of Nebraska, to the Salt Lake Valley, cooking their nightly meals in their Dutch ovens fueled by the burning of dried buffalo manure.

I've read accounts explaining that the wives would mix the bread dough in the morning and put it in the Dutch ovens, which were placed in the carts. By evening the dough would have risen and would be ready to bake.

In the later 1800s, Dutch ovens were also vital parts of the chuck wagons on the famous cattle drives of the West.

1900s

In the 1900s, as the technology and affordability of indoor stoves and ranges increased, Dutch ovens fell out of use. Cast iron was still popular, particularly in skillets. Dutch ovens lost their legs and became more of the range-top ware and roaster pots for which they are popular now.

Still, traditional Dutch ovens remained popular among campers, hunters, hikers, and other outdoor enthusiasts.

In 1985 the International Dutch Oven Society (IDOS) was formed in Utah, "with the goals to preserve and promote the skills and art of Dutch Oven cooking. From its humble beginnings in the Rocky Mountains, IDOS has grown to its current status as the largest and most productive group of black pot enthusiasts in the world" (http://www.idos.org/AboutUs.php).

2000 AND BEYOND

Dutch ovening as a hobby continues to grow. A few adjustments to the traditional designs have been coming out in the last few years, even since the 1990s, including the Ultimate Dutch Oven, manufactured by Camp Chef, which features a hollow cone in the center of the oven to allow hot air to enter, convection style. Many of these ovens also include a small hole in the lip of the lid for the insertion of thermometers or thermometer leads. Maca makes big, deep Dutch ovens, many shaped in ovals to better accommodate large turkeys.

I find it interesting to reflect on the changes in cooking technology. Now we have glass-top ranges, microwave ovens, convection ovens, ovens that clean themselves, automatic timers, tabletop grills, panini makers, and a million other modern ways to cook. A Dutch oven–cooked meal is delicious, nutritious, and wonderful. But this is not always the quickest or easiest way to cook. I cook in Dutch ovens because it's my hobby and because it's fun. We have contests and parties that celebrate Dutch oven cooking. In the back of my head, though, I keep the haunting thought: my ancestors used it to feed their families every day. Over the years, the Dutch oven has developed for very practical reasons: it worked.

SEASONING THE DUTCH OVEN

You'll hear a lot of talk in this book and among Dutch oven chefs about "seasoning" and "patina." These are really the same thing: that deep, rich, black coating that builds up on a Dutch oven over time and keeps the iron from rusting and the food from sticking. I'm dead serious when I say that a well-seasoned Dutch oven is a better nonstick pan than most with Teflon.

The patina is made from carbonized oils. The heat bakes layer after layer of carbonized oil into the pores of the iron. I've also read that patina makes for better heat transfer from the pot to the food.

As I mentioned before, most manufacturers season their Dutch ovens in the factory, but many brands still sell their ovens unseasoned. You may also manage to acquire an old oven that needs reseasoning. From time to time, I'll reseason mine.

First of all, the Dutch oven needs to be prepared. If it's new and unseasoned, it will probably be coated with a layer of wax to keep it from rusting. You can scrub this off using hot tap water.

If this is a rescued piece, you might have to scrub more intensely. We mentioned in the last step not to clean your Dutch oven using metal scrapers, scrubbers, or harsh detergents because they will take off the patina. At this point, you can use any of those because the whole point is to take off any of the old patina and any rust.

You have many options for seasoning cast iron. You're going to be heating up oil until it literally burns onto the surface of the metal, so there's going to be smoke. For that reason, I like to do it outdoors in my gas grill.

I start by firing up my grill and removing the upper-level grill racks to make room for the Dutch ovens. I have a thermometer on the lid of my grill, so the temperature is easy to track (assuming it's accurate). My goal is to heat it up to 400 degrees. More about that later. I put the pot part of the Dutch oven upside down without the lid on the grill. I set the lid on the legs of the upturned pot. I then let them heat up with the grill lid down to trap the heat.

When they're at 350 degrees, climbing up to 400, I pull the Dutch oven off the grill and set it on my back porch. I spread a layer of shortening over it, inside and out, lid and legs and all. Putting on the grease is tricky because the pot is hot. If I'm not careful, I can end up touching the pot a little and get zinged. This happens especially if the melted shortening soaks through the paper towel or cloth I'm using to spread it.

Once they're coated, I put the pots back on the grill the same way as they'd been heating up, and I close the lid again.

After about 20 minutes, I open the grill; the pot has a smooth, black patina on it. Then, I turn off the gas and leave the lid open for it to cool just a little. After a few minutes, while the Dutch oven is still quite hot, I pull it off the grill and coat it again in another thin layer of shortening.

Then I leave the oven on the back porch to fully cool. If you want, you can do a third or even a fourth coating. I find that doing two coats is fine, especially considering that the patina will continue to build with each use.

ADDITIONAL DUTCH OVEN GEAR

In lesson one, we talked about some of the basic gear you need to cook. Now let's talk a bit about some additional items you can buy that will make things a little bit easier for you but are not as necessary. Be aware of these items but also know that you can make great dishes and wonderful food without them. Don't spend a ton of money until you know what you really need or want.

TABLES

You can purchase and use several different cooking surfaces, which I mentioned in the last lesson. One is a low metal table, about a foot or so high. It keeps the heat up off the ground and means that you don't have to stoop down quite as far. They're also easy to disassemble and transport, they can support a lot of weight, and they're good for stacking ovens. I like them a lot.

You can also find adjustable metal tables that are much higher. They raise the level of the Dutch oven to waist height. They come in varying widths as well: some will fit two ovens side by side, others will fit three. Many even have removable wind screens. I also like the screen, but they're more money.

LID REST/TRIVET

Sometimes, when you lift the lid, you want to do things to the food, and sometimes that takes two hands. Where are you going to put the lid while you're working? Don't set it on the ground; this will get the underside dirty, and then that dirt falls into the food.

A lid rest is a small metal stand, raised off the ground a bit, that you can use to set the lid on. It's not complicated, but it does have a couple of other great uses. You can put the lid rest in the center of a circle of coals, with the lid inverted on top of it. Then you can use the heated lid as a griddle for pancakes, bacon, eggs, or tortillas. My son used this strategy to make crepes, much to my surprise.

WHISK BRUSH

When you're doing meals with long cooking times, like roasts and such (something I'll talk about in future lessons), as you're replenishing the coals above and below your Dutch oven, you'll begin to accumulate thick piles of ash. It's good to dust that stuff away, because it can actually lessen the heat transfer, and it can also block airflow underneath. To accomplish this, a good hand whisk brush is what you need.

Here's the hard part: it must be a natural-reed brush. Plastic bristles will melt almost right away as you use them around the hot coals and hot lid. The natural bristles will singe, but they won't melt or burn. These brushes aren't expensive—a few bucks—but I have a hard time finding them. I've checked all of the supermarkets, megastores, and dollar stores all around my area, and they're just not to be found. A few places online sell them, though.

CHIMNEY

A chimney is a pretty common item to find, and most people are probably familiar with it, especially if they've ever done any charcoal grilling. It's a metal cylinder with holes, particularly at the base, and some sort of mesh or holey metal barrier about a third of the way up on the inside. It will also have some kind of handle structure attached to the side.

The idea is that you can put a few bits of newspaper in the space under the barrier, put some charcoal briquettes above it, and light the newspaper. The flames from the newspaper will light the charcoal, and the rising hot air (flowing through the holes in the base) will carry the heat and flames upward to light the upper coals. The aim is to light your coals without using the harsh chemical accelerants like lighter fluid.

Now, I've always had some troubles with the ones I've bought. I can't seem to get them to light well. The newspaper burns away, and the coals still aren't lit. So I still end up using lighter fluid.

I have, however, heard a few suggestions to make it work better.

One is to liberally drizzle the newspaper with some cooking oil. I'm told this will make the paper burn longer. Another idea is to keep some instant-light charcoal on hand and to put a few briquettes at the bottom of your chimney first.

I also suspect that if there are holes up the side of your chimney, it will have better ventilation.

I do like a couple of things about the chimney, and that's why I use one anyway. It holds the heat in a nice column, so the coals get white a bit quicker. It's also a great way to keep fresh coals going. I simply keep a few burning coals in the bottom of the chimney. I add a dozen or so fresh coals and mix them up. In fifteen minutes or so, I have more coals to replenish my Dutch ovens.

I've also developed a cool method of shaking the chimney so as to rotate the coals, allowing more even burning. With a flick of the wrist, I shake the chimney upward, tossing the coals forward to back and turning them over.

GLOVES

Heavy gloves are very useful when handling hot things. They are convenient when lifting a Dutch oven or trying to empty it out. Simple hot pads can work too, but having the protection actually *on* your hands means that you don't have to worry about slipping. Several Dutch oven companies make heavy leather gloves; you can find them in hardware stores all over.

WINDSCREENS

Windscreens are simply panels of sheet metal hinged together. The idea is that you can stand it up on end on the windward side of the Dutch ovens, and it will block (or at least slow) the wind on breezy days. Even though windscreens are available commercially, I've seen a lot of people do some pretty amazing improvisations on this idea. One of the cleverest was a bunch of old license plates all hinged together with wire loops.

A lot of the tall tables made for Dutch ovening have windscreens built in.

TRIPOD

This is a great tool if you want to make a soup or chili over an open, active fire. The tall, metal tripod has a chain hanging down that hooks to the bail wire of the Dutch oven. You can easily adjust the heat by adjusting the length of the chain.

HOOD/DOME

My in-laws, when they saw my interest in Dutch ovening, bought me a hood. It's a large, metal cylinder, capped off at the top. There are holes around the bottom, and an adjustable vent at the top. The idea is to use it to cover the Dutch ovens as they cook, trapping even more heat and protecting the coals from the wind.

The particular model they got for me wasn't designed well, honestly. I don't think it had enough holes in the base, and the circulation wasn't good. I've used this enclosure at times and it actually put out my coals.

It does, however, come in handy when I'm cooking and it starts raining. I raise it up on a couple of bricks to increase the gap at the bottom for the air. It's big enough to cover two 12-inch, shallow ovens stacked on top of each other.

I've also seen hoods made of heat-resistant textiles used in much the same way. Mostly, however, these are designed for using a Dutch oven over a propane stove. In theory, it traps the heat so that upper coals are not necessary.

I KNOW of many, many more options for additional gear. Dutch oven liners, tote bags, even Christmas tree ornaments. Believe me, if you have money to spend, then someone somewhere is willing to take it from you. In most cases, you'll get something good for your money, but always ask yourself if you really *need* the item you're spending all that cash on. I remind myself that my ancestors didn't have any of that, and they still cooked well.

DUTCH OVEN COBBLERS AND DUMP CAKES

Ah, the humble cobbler. It almost never fails. Whenever I tell people I love to cook in Dutch ovens, their eyes get wistful, and their countenances become almost angelic. Then they say something like, "Oh, I remember once I had the most delicious dessert out of a Dutch oven! It was at a campout [or cookout, or whatever] at [somewhere or someone's]! It had peaches and cake. We ate it with ice cream, and it was incredible!"

It doesn't matter how complex and intricate my dishes may be or how they rate on the gourmet scale—they will never compare to that delicious cobbler that Great-Uncle Wilbur makes with the cake mixes and the canned peaches!

They're also called "dump cakes" because you dump everything in and bake it up. It really doesn't get much simpler than that!

Let me make a confession: I used to dislike cooking dump cake cobblers.

But you have to do it! It's a Dutch oven tradition. You put some canned peaches with their juice in the bottom of the Dutch oven, and then you shake a cake mix on top. Sometimes you put butter on top of the floating mix. The juices boil up and mingle with the cake mix as the cobbler cooks, and the butter (if used) melts down into the bubbling mire. Cool it (just a little) and serve it up with ice cream.

Let me reiterate—I've never really liked to cook dump cake cobblers. I've been of that opinion for two reasons: (1) Everybody does them. I mean e-v-e-r-y-b-o-d-y.

And that leads me to the next reason: (2) For the longest time, I couldn't do them! They never turned out the way I wanted them to. They were either too runny and sloppy, or the cake mix never mixed, resulting in dried-out powder on top. I mean, the recipe couldn't get any easier, yet it didn't seem to work for me.

I figured that two issues were preventing me from getting the perfect dump cake cobbler each time. One was the balance of peach syrup to how much cake mix was on top, and the other was the placement of the heat to make it boil up properly.

Part of the problem in the past was that, since everybody does these desserts, everybody does them just a little differently. So resolving the issue by research didn't get me anywhere. I had to experiment. Then one Sunday, I think I found the balance of all the factors. It was perfect! The crust on top was an actual crusty cake, not a runny paste and not a dry powder. The peaches on the bottom were nicely blended in with their own saucy syrup. It tasted great!

MARK'S VERSION OF THE DUTCH OVEN DUMP CAKE COBBLER

TOOLS
12-inch, shallow Dutch oven
12 coals below
12 coals above

INGREDIENTS
2 (16-oz.) cans peaches in light syrup
2 (18-oz.) boxes yellow cake mix
¼ cup brown sugar
liberal shakes of cinnamon, nutmeg
1 stick butter

I START (AFTER lighting up some coals) by opening the cans of peaches and pouring them, with the syrup, directly into the Dutch oven. Then I sprinkle the cake mix over the peaches and syrup.

After many tries, I've decided that there should be a 1:1 ratio between cans of syrup and boxes of cake mix. I also discovered that one box of cake mix is not enough in a 12-inch Dutch oven. If I were doing this in a 10-inch Dutch oven, I would halve everything.

Then I crumble the brown sugar over the top of the cake mix and sprinkle on the spices. I cut the stick of butter into small pieces and scatter that over the crust as well. Then the lid goes on, and the whole Dutch oven goes on the coals.

Now, if I were baking a normal dessert, I would put more coals on top and fewer coals on the bottom. That's how you're supposed to do things when you're baking. In this case, however, I want more heat on the bottom to get the peach juice boiling up to blend with the cake mix. So I lay out about 12 fresh, hot coals in a circle and set the Dutch oven on it. Then I put just as many coals on top. If it's cold or breezy out, then I might put a couple of extra coals on the top and bottom, up to 14.

I bake it for about 35 minutes before checking it, rotating it once along the way. Honestly, I'm not really certain how to tell if it's done, other than the rich smell. I just look for a nice gold on the top crust, and some syrup boiling action. I let it cook a bit longer than it looks like it needs. I've always figured cobbler is hard to burn, so it won't hurt to give it another 10 minutes or so if I'm not certain.

Then I take it off the coals and bring it in to let it cool some. This not only keeps it from burning my guests' mouths, but it also gives the boiling syrup and the cake mix even more time to settle together. Finally, top it with ice cream or whipped cream and eat!

SO NOW I like to do the dump cake cobblers! I can do them exactly as I had always wanted them, with a nice crust on top, a little syrupy blend underneath, and delicious peaches as a base. The sugar and the butter add a little crispiness and flavor, and the spices just take it to a new level.

Now that I've figured cobblers out, they truly *are* easy. And they satisfy! If I'm bustin' my back making the most elaborate of dinners, I can count on a simple cobbler to finish it off with ease and style.

Dump cake cobblers come in many different varieties and flavors. Here's another one I've done and enjoyed.

BLACK FOREST CHOCOLATE DUMP CAKE

TOOLS
12-inch Dutch oven

12 coals below
12 coals above

INGREDIENTS
2 cans cherry pie filling
1 can non-diet cola (I prefer Dr Pepper)
2 boxes chocolate cake mix
a little bit of brown sugar
½ cup chopped pecans
1 cube butter

I START by pouring the cans of cherry pie filling in the bottom of the oven and spreading the contents around. Then I pour in the can of cola. Pie fillings don't have as much liquid as canned peaches, so you'll need to add more. That's where the cola comes in. It also adds a wonderful flavor. On top of that, I sprinkle and spread the chocolate cake mix.

I sprinkle on a few crumbs of brown sugar and then toss on the nuts. Finally, I cut the butter into small chunks and space them over the top.

That's it. Then I put the oven on the coals and bake for 30–40 minutes like before.

You could do more variations by simply using different cake mixes and fruits. How about a couple of cans of apple pie filling, with a lemon-lime soda? I would still use a yellow cake, and the cinnamon and nutmeg too. How about a strawberry short-cake? Use a white cake, strawberry filling, a cherry soda, cinnamon, and cocoa powder! Mint leaves would taste great as a garnish on that one!

CLEANUP
This will clean up the same way as the other dish will, with the exception that with sugary and syrupy things, bits may have baked onto the side of the Dutch oven. For that, there is a very useful tool called a "pot scraper." It's a simple plastic square with a slightly rounded corner and a slightly sharpened edge that you can use to scrape out some of the more resistant bits of caked-on sugar.

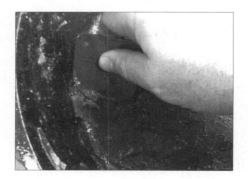

As always, it's good to clean the Dutch oven as soon as you're done with it. If left for later, food can eat away at the patina, especially if the food is acidic like fruits or tomatoes. At the very least, the food can become glued on.

CONGRATULATIONS! YOU'VE just cooked, served, and cleaned up after your first Dutch oven dessert! Another great accomplishment! Take a minute to feel good about that. Also, take a minute to analyze and see what you've learned.

REVIEW

You learned

- where Dutch ovens came from and about the rich heritage they carry;
- which tools and accessories you can buy to make Dutch ovening easier; and
- how to make a delicious, traditional dessert.

ANALYSIS QUESTIONS

How did the cobbler taste?

How were the spices and flavorings you used?

Was the crust done to your liking?

What would you do differently next time?

BASIC CHEFFERY

CHILI

WHEN I cook the dishes that I present on marksblackpot.com, for the most part I'm cooking on my back porch rather than out in the wild at a campout or in a park as part of a cook-off. So, I'm using my regular kitchen counter for food prep, and I have a good stock of kitchen tools and utensils. If, however, you're preparing to cook "on the road" or if you're just learning how to cook for yourself, here are some things you'll need.

TABLE

As I said, I'm usually using my own regular kitchen counter for ingredient preparation, and then I take the ingredients out to the porch to cook. If you're cooking anywhere that's not in your house, you'll need to make sure that you have a surface for prep.

A good, solid folding table will work. I don't like card tables because they're not that stable, so they make me nervous with a heavy Dutch oven on them. Most commercial folding tables aren't very high, but some are adjustable. There are also a lot of commercially available tables specifically designed to be portable camping cook stations. I've seen simple ones for 50 dollars or even less, and elaborate ones that even have dishwashing stations built in for 150 dollars or more.

MEASURING TOOLS

A lot of these things will go without saying, but I'm going to say them anyway. Get a good set of measuring cups and spoons. Know the difference between measuring cups for liquid and those for powders. In powders, the contents are measured fully to the top of the cup, so that you can scoop out the powder, scrape it off level, and have the exact measure you need. In liquid measuring, the cup will be clear and marked on the side, almost to the top, so you can pour in the liquid, see when it reaches the correct volume, and then move it to the mixing point without spilling it. You'll need both types.

MIXING BOWLS

I own a lot of these, and I only use them for mixing some of the time. Most of the time I use them for carrying the chopped or otherwise prepared ingredients from the prep area to the Dutch ovens. I would recommend getting at least 3–4 of these. I like the plastic ones better, but I'm not really sure why.

WHISK

A good, classic wire whisk is essential. I like ones with firmer wires. A plastic coating will keep it from scratching the patina on your Dutch oven.

STIRRING, SAMPLING, AND SERVING SPOONS

You'll want to have a nice collection of spoons. Get some wooden ones for stirring. Not only do they not scratch the patina, but they are also strong enough to hold up to a good bread dough. They're usually not deep enough or angled right to scoop up a taste, so for that I recommend a basic table spoon or a bigger metal or plastic serving spoon. I prefer metal. If you use a plastic spoon and lean it on the edge of the hot Dutch oven, the spoon handle will sometimes melt. For serving, get solid spoons and some with holes in the bowl. Getting a spatula and a turner or two is a good idea too.

SEASONINGS

In lesson six, I'll cover herbs and spices in much greater detail. For now, you'll just want some basics. Salt and pepper are obvious choices. Lately, I've been discovering just how much I like grinders for both salt and pepper. Another staple for me is paprika. I like to have garlic powder for when I don't have fresh garlic or for other situations. I don't like garlic salt because I prefer to add the individual ingredients separately to the exact amounts that I like rather than relying on the garlic salt blend. I always like a bit of chili powder too, not necessarily for heat but for a bit of zest. Over time, you can decide what you like.

THERMOMETERS

Cooking thermometers are critical, especially for breads and meats. It can be tricky to tell when they're done simply by the look or the taste. A quick temperature read will tell you when it's safe to eat and when it's cooked the way you want it to be. You don't need an expensive, fancy digital readout. They're nice but not necessary.

Get one that can stand up to the heat of the oven, one that you can leave stuck in the meat or the loaf of bread as it finishes. And once you've found a brand and model that you trust, buy a caseload of them, because then you won't have to keep looking for them!

CUTTING BOARD

I've tried a lot of cutting surfaces, and my favorite is a thick, heavy wood cutting board. I especially like the ones that look like checkerboards from the top because that means the woodgrain is running with the knife and it's "self healing." The plastic ones are easier to carry, but they move on the tabletop when I get rockin' with the knife. You decide.

KNIVES

This is a good time to turn our attention to the one kitchen tool that I've learned to trust and value above all others: the knife. With a simple set of three quality knives, you can do almost anything in the kitchen, and you can get rid of all of those pointless "handy kitchen gadgets" that you've acquired all these years. These are all useless unitaskers that just take up space, and with a good knife and some good knife skills, you can throw 'em all away.

The three knives you'll need are a paring knife, a long carving knife, and the star of your whole kitchen: a high-quality chef's knife.

You can spend hundreds of dollars for those fancy sets of knives that will cut leather and soda cans and nails and sit in a nice wooden storage block, or you can spend less money more carefully and get the three knives you need: ones that will cut food well.

First, before I talk about how to shop for a great knife, let's talk about the parts.

The Blade
The whole metal part that you cut with.

The Handle
The part (usually nonmetal) you hold on to.

The Edge
The sharp part all along the blade that cuts your food, or your fingers if you're not careful.

The Tip
The sharp, pointy end of the knife, used for detailed cutting.

The Spine
The dull part of the blade that's opposite the edge.

The Bolster
The metal part between the handle and the blade.

The Heel
The part of the blade that extends below the handle and the bolster, to the edge.

The Tang
The metal extension of the blade that goes through the handle in better-quality knives.

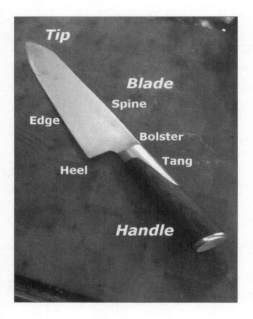

NOW THAT you know the proper terms, you can go out shopping for a good knife. As you're looking around, you can use certain tests that will show if a knife is a good one to use. Trust me, I've used good and bad knives, and there *is* a difference.

THE KNUCKLE TEST
If you hold the knife in your hand and put the edge of the blade on the cutting block, as if you're cutting something, the heel and the bolster need to be deep enough that you're not knocking your knuckles on the board.

THE TRIANGLE TEST

The shape of a cross section of the blade should be a triangle. By that, I mean that from the spine of the blade to the cutting edge should be smooth. It shouldn't need a bevel to make it sharp.

THE STIFFNESS TEST

The blade should be pretty stiff, bending little, if at all.

THE BALANCE TEST

If you hold the blade horizontally and balance it on your finger, the balance point should be at about the bolster, maybe even a bit into the blade.

FINALLY, THE BUDGET TEST

It shouldn't cost too much. You can pay upwards of hundreds of dollars for a single chef's knife. Not only is that probably out of most people's budget, but it would also be a bit like a beginner violinist playing a Stradivarius. If you look for a knife that will pass these tests, you can probably pick one up for anywhere from twenty to fifty dollars.

I have an 8-inch chef's knife that I love, and it cost me only twenty dollars.

I'm much less picky about my other knives. The paring knife should fit easily into the curled fingers of your hand, with plenty of blade (at least 3 inches or so) to feed the food onto. A carving knife should be long and narrow, so you can get around bones if you need to. Often, I confess, I'll just use my chef's knife for carving too.

Now, to get some mad cookin' skillz in th' kitchen, yo . . .

DUTCH OVEN CHILI FROM SCRATCH, NOT CANS

One time, my church had a chili cook-off, and a lot of people brought their best chili. I was amazed at how much variety there was. Some chili had beans; others didn't. Some had meat; others didn't. One even had noodles. But somehow they were each called chili. At the end, after everyone had tasted the various chilis, they gave out awards. They had to come up with enough awards for everyone to have one so that, in the end, everyone came away with a smile. Some of the awards, however, were a bit comical. One was "Most Creative Use of a Can Opener."

Ultimately, it's true that if you want chili, you can just open up a can, pour it out, and heat it up. This is what I do when I want a quick lunch. Or you can open up cans of ingredients, mix them together, and heat that up. That can involve a little more creativity, but the chili's still not fresh.

What I want to teach in this lesson is how to make a delicious chili completely from scratch—from fresh, or at least uncanned, ingredients. There are a couple of reasons for this. First, I think fresh tastes the best. Second, I'm going to use this as a vehicle to teach you a lot of good, basic culinary skills as they relate specifically to the Dutch oven.

I'm going to show you four basic cuts with your knives: the chop, the slice, the mince, and paring/peeling. I'm going to show you how to use these to prepare onions, green peppers, and other ingredients. I'm also going to teach you how to use your Dutch oven for three cooking techniques: browning, sautéing, and simmering. You can make easier chilis than this. For example, you could use ground beef instead of a small roast. You could use canned beans and canned tomatoes. And it would still taste good. But then, you wouldn't learn how to slice up the meat or how to peel and dice the tomatoes or how to zest the lemon, would you?

Once you've learned these basic skills, you'll be amazed how often you use them in many other dishes of all kinds. If you were building a house, this would be where you would learn how to swing a hammer and push a saw.

And, by the way, I'll show you how to do these things in such a way that you get to keep all ten of your fingers. Bonus!

INGREDIENTS

1–2 lbs. beef, not ground. Maybe a couple of steaks. If you use a roast, you won't use it all. That's okay.

1–2 lbs. dried, bagged beans. I like to mix it up, visually, and use a couple of different types, like kidney beans and black-eyed peas, for example, or pinto and black beans.

cooking oil. Personally, I like EVOO (extra virgin olive oil). Any kind of veggie oil will do.

1 fresh head of garlic—a bunch of cloves all wrapped up in the paper that Mother Nature gave them.

2–3 medium to large onions. Yellow, preferably, as they're the most flavorful in soups and stews.

3 sweet peppers. I like to do a green one, a yellow one, and a red one. I can't tell a difference in the taste, but the colors look really cool!

3 celery stalks. Save the leaves from the tender inner stalks too.

2–3 medium to large tomatoes

6–8 cups water and/or chicken stock in any amount or combination. Chicken stock is the only ingredient I'll allow you to use from a can or a package. I like to make my own stock, but that's a whole other lesson. Someday . . .

salt and pepper

1–2 lemons

1–2 jalapeños (or use chili powder as an alternative)

cumin

fresh cilantro leaves

fresh celery leaves. I told you not to forget them!

SUPPLIES

For supplies, you'll want one 12-inch, shallow (or deep, if you're gonna feed a lot of people) Dutch oven and a full 20-pound bag of charcoal briquettes. You probably won't use it all, but if you start with half a bag, you might run out, and that wouldn't be good.

This dish will also take some time, so it's not the thing to throw together at the last minute when you come home from work. Take some time on a Saturday or Sunday to really go through the steps and learn the processes.

SOAKING THE BEANS

At least 4–6 hours before cooking, open up the bags of beans and put them into one of your mixing bowls. Sometimes I'll do this overnight. You really don't need all of both bags, maybe ½ to ⅔ of each. Again, I like to mix them for visual variety. Put in a lot of water, enough to cover the beans and a few inches more. The beans will soak up a lot of the water. That's the point.

If you're not doing an overnight soak, this would be a good time to also start thawing the meat if it's frozen.

CHOPPING THE CELERY

Next, we're going to start preparing the vegetables. This can be done right before cooking or hours before with the results stored in baggies in the fridge. Here, also, is where we'll begin learning the basic cuts with the chef's knife. We'll start with the cut called "the chop." Before we do, though, break off a few stalks of celery and rinse them off.

First, we'll learn how to hold a chef's knife. Use whichever hand is dominant. I'm a righty, so that's what the pictures will show. Grip the blade between the index finger and the thumb, pinching the blade just on the metal side of the bolster. The rest of the fingers wrap around the handle. It looks like this:

Grab the celery and, holding the knife properly, cut off the tips right below the upper branches and cut off the bottoms where it starts to flare out and go white. It's a bit easier to handle the celery if you cut all the stalks in half at this point.

The off-hand grip is very important (by "off hand," I mean the hand that will not have the knife. Since I'm a righty, my left hand is the off hand). The off hand will guide both the blade and the food. Using the proper grip, or hand shape, will ensure that you'll finish your task with all of your fingertips still on your fingers.

Hold your hand up in the air and make a bear claw. It helps to actually growl when you do this. Trust me. Then, draw your fingers closer to the palm of your hand, flattening and tightening the bear claw grip. It looks like this:

Then put the claw on the stacked up celery sticks so that the sticks are pointing outward, away from your fingers, but not too far. Like this:

Now, bring your blade hand up and place the edge on the celery. The flat side of the blade should rest against the first two knuckles of the off hand. The handle of the knife should be raised so that the knife is not yet cutting into the celery, but the tip of the knife is resting on the cutting board. Because of the bear claw, your fingertips are curled under, nicely avoiding contact with the edge of the knife.

Keeping the tip of the knife on the board, slide the knife forward and downward. This forward and downward motion both slices through the celery and chops down through it.

Lift the blade a little by the handle so that the tip is still on the board and the edge is just above the celery. The flat of the blade is still resting against your knuckles, and the edge doesn't rise above them. Use your thumb to push about a quarter inch of celery under the blade. While you're lifting the blade, also move it back to its original position. Then drop it down for another cut.

With a bit of practice, you coordinate the circular motion of the blade hand with the feeding motion of the off hand. The knuckles guide the blade, and the curled fingers avoid the edge.

Put the chopped celery into one of the mixing bowls I mentioned a while before.

This technique is not always easy to grasp. But after some practice with a few ingredients and dishes, you'll be whipping along like a pro—*whack, whack, whack.* Notice that the pieces of celery are all about the same size. Consistent size means consistent cooking.

SLICING THE ONIONS

There are lots of ways to cut up an onion. This is the way I like to do it for stews and chilis, where you'll want larger pieces. To begin with, we need to start with a cut called "the slice." This is actually an easier cut to do than the chop. The blade hand grip is the same, but two off-hand grips are used. One is the bear claw, like I showed before, and the other is one I call the "overhand." We'll start with that one.

Knock the loose skin off the onion and put the onion on the chopping block. Imagine that the root spot and the stalk part are like the north and south poles of the onion. We're going to slice longitudinally, cutting right across both of these points.

Grip the knife and place it with the tip on the board and the handle raised above the onion so that the knife looks like it's going to cut that way. Reaching over the spine of the knife, grip the onion between your fingers and thumb. If the onion moved in the process of setting the knife, you can adjust it for the correct longitudinal cut. Your fingers should be well clear of the cut. Here's what it should look like:

Keeping the blade on the board, pull the knife toward you and downward, cutting completely through the onion.

The big difference between the chop and the slice is that the cutting motion of the slice is with the handle pulling toward you, while in the chop it's pushing forward, away from you. Also, a slice is a single cut, while the chop is a fluid motion with lots of cuts. Easily 80 percent of all the knife work you do in your cooking will be one of these two.

Set one half of the onion, sliced-side down, back on the chopping block. Turn it so that the stalk end is pointing toward your blade hand. Using a bear claw grip with the off hand and setting the flat side of the blade against the knuckles again, use a slice to cut this end off.

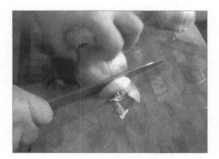

Then turn the onion around and, using the bear claw again, slice off the root end. Pick up the onion and peel off the top layer (the dried onion skin and even the top fresh layer, if necessary). Discard the peeled skin and the two sliced-off ends. Put the now-peeled onion back on the cutting board, sliced-side down, and slice it in half again, longitudinally, using the overhand grip.

The last step is to chop the onion latitudinally. Reposition the onion 90 degrees, sliced-side down, with the sliced-off pole ends facing the blade. Using your bear claw grip and the chop technique, cut the onion into ¼-inch slices as shown:

Put the onions into a mixing bowl, ready for the cooking! Now you've learned two fundamental cuts in the culinary world! That's a real accomplishment! As you start to watch other people cook, you'll be surprised how few people know how to do this. You'll also be surprised how quick and easy this method makes food preparation. There's a reason they use these techniques in restaurants.

SLICING AND DICING THE PEPPERS

Now we're going to practice it some more, on some veggies that don't make you cry. Get the peppers ready! Rinse them off and put one of them on the cutting board, stem up.

You'll notice bulges and indents all around the perimeter of the pepper. When you cut it open, you see that the indents are the white spines that connect to the center core. These white spines are not so tasty. To cut around them, position the knife to make a slice from one indent across to another. Use either the bear claw or the overhand grip, whichever you prefer. I'd probably use the bear claw.

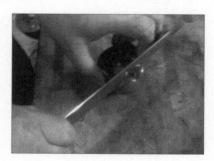

Make the slice, cutting just to the side of the adjacent indentations. It should look like this:

Continue around the pepper, making similar slices. You're cutting away the tasty green flesh of the pepper and leaving the core and the spines in one intact piece. Then you can just throw away the core.

Now, you'll use long slices to cut these pepper pieces into strips. Stack them or cut them one at a time; it doesn't matter. I would recommend using the bear claw grip for this step.

Finally, turn the sliced strips of pepper like you had the celery and chop them into small squares, nicely diced. You can put these into the same mixing bowl as the onions.

By the time you get through with these three veggies, you'll probably feel more comfortable with the cutting techniques.

PEELING AND MINCING THE GARLIC

Working with fresh garlic is so much fun. Not only does it taste good, but it's also so fun to mince that I wonder why anyone would want to use pre-minced garlic. This is the third cutting technique.

But first we must prepare the cloves. Break off 4–5 cloves from the head and set them to the side on the cutting board. Get one of them and hold it up. You'll see that it has a natural curve to it. Put it on the cutting board so that the curve is convex, like a bubble facing upward.

Put the flat side of your chef's knife on top of the clove, pressing it down a bit.

Using the butt of your hand, smack the knife and flatten the garlic. Go ahead, give it a good whack. This action will loosen the papery shell and make it easy to peel. Yeah, it might squash the garlic, but then you're going to mince it anyway, right? Eventually, with practice, you'll get a feel for how hard to hit it.

With the rind broken, it's pretty easy to peel off the skin. Do this with the other cloves and gather them together into a pile in the middle of the cutting board. Here we go with the mince.

Using the same grip as before in your blade hand, put the tip of the knife on the board, just beyond the garlic, with the handle raised. It should look like you're about to slice them. Place the palm of the off hand on the spine of the blade, near the tip, with the fingers and thumb stretched out, safely away from the blade.

Bring the handle down, cutting the garlic, and begin rocking back and forth, like a seesaw, between your two hands. Turn the knife and your hands as you're doing so to cut more pieces of garlic.

Every few seconds, pause to regather the garlic pieces and reposition them to get better cutting angles. Keep cutting until the garlic is as finely minced as you want. Finer minces result in a stronger garlic flavor. More and smaller pieces also make it easier for the garlic to mix into the overall dish and spread the flavor more evenly.

Congratulations! You've mastered three of the basic cuts. One more.

PEELING, PARING, AND DICING THE TOMATOES

The last step in the preparation of the vegetables is the tomatoes. There are, frankly, better ways to peel a tomato than the following; some are even a bit quicker, and others leave more usable tomato flesh. However, this way is simple, and it will help you learn the final basic culinary cut: that of paring. This is the only cut that happens off the board and also the only one where the edge of the blade faces you. Since it's the food and not the knife that moves, you're safe.

Using your blade hand, make a pistol in the air with your fingers, like you did when you were a little kid playing Cowboys and Indians. I guess that's not politically correct anymore, right? Do it anyway. Put the handle of the paring knife in the three fingers of the blade hand that are curled toward your palm. The blade edge will point toward your palm, and the thumb will rest against the barrel finger of the pistol, which will still be extended. The thumb is up and will guide the food.

Pick up the tomato with the off hand and, beginning at the top, introduce it to the blade. Turning the tomato with your off hand, and guiding it with your thumb, you begin to peel off thin layers of the skin. Try to cut away as little of the flesh as possible. Notice that the blade hand doesn't cut into the fruit, but rather the off hand moves the fruit into the blade. This will keep the knife from slipping and cutting either hand. You can use a gentle up and down motion of the blade hand to slice into the tomato to get it started.

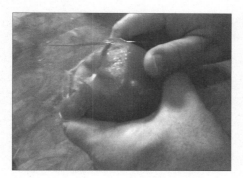

Once all of the tomatoes are peeled, place one on the cutting board, and ready your chef's knife in the blade hand. Using the overhand grip, slice it in half, "pole to pole" as you did the onion. Put one half, sliced-side down, on the cutting board.

Still using the overhand grip, slice the tomato into ¼-inch slices latitudinally, like the onion. Then turn it 90 degrees and slice it again. The overhand grip helps to hold the disintegrating tomato in place. Be careful to keep your fingers clear of the blade.

Then cut the other half of the tomato, followed by the other tomatoes. Put them in their own mixing bowl.

Now you know all of the basic cuts! You can chop, slice, dice, mince, and pare! You are on your way to culinary stardom, wealth, and fame. Or at least the admiration of those you cook for. Using the proper technique with a good sharp knife is more than just quick, easy, and visually impressive; it also cuts the food with less damage and tearing of the cells, so it cooks better. If the pieces are cut evenly and to a consistent size, they will also cook more evenly and in the same amount of time. Your food will not only look better but it will also taste better.

SLICING THE MEAT

Now it's time for the meat. It should be thawed and patted dry. Rinse off your cutting board. Since we did the veggies first, it's not necessary to sanitize the board to prevent cross-contamination. Still, it wouldn't hurt to wash it off.

We're going to cube the meat into ¾-inch to 1-inch chunks. If you'll need to make longer cuts to make that happen, you might want to use your carving knife. If not, your chef's knife will do just fine.

First, cut away any bones and fat chunks. If you're using a big roast, cut off a 1-inch-thick slice. Then with a bear claw grip, use the slice to cut that piece into strips about an inch wide. Turn it 90 degrees and slice it again, making cubes.

That's it. Really. Put the meat cubes into a mixing bowl, sprinkle on some salt and pepper, and stir it all up. Set it aside.

Light the coals and prep the Dutch oven for browning

Okay, all the food is ready! It's time to start cooking! Just to refresh your memory, We're going to learn three Dutch oven cooking techniques: browning, sautéing, and simmering.

Begin by lighting up 25–30 coals, which would be enough to fill a typical chimney starter about ¾ of the way to the top. As it lights, shake it or mix the coals to get a good, even white edge on all the coals.

Pour some oil (maybe a tablespoon) in the bottom of your Dutch oven and, using a paper towel, spread the oil around, up the sides, and all over.

Shake out 20–25 lit coals onto your cooking surface and spread them around. We'll be using all bottom heat for this dish. Hold your hand about a foot above the coals and feel the heat. Make a mental note of what that feels like. Put the Dutch oven over the coals with the lid on and let it heat up. After about 10–15 minutes, take off the lid and put another tablespoon of oil in the bottom. Tip the Dutch oven to spread the oil around. Soon, the surface of the oil will start to "shimmer," indicating that it's heated up. You don't want it to smoke, but you want it to be very hot.

BROWNING THE MEAT

Toss in the meat chunks. They should start to sizzle immediately. Stir them up with one of those wooden spoons we talked about earlier. Let the meat cook, but not for very long. The idea is to get a good, brown sear on the sides of the meat. At this stage, cooking the meat through is not critical. If the Dutch oven is hot enough, the meat should sear within a few minutes. When that's done, pull the meat out and put it back into the mixing bowl.

SAUTÉING THE VEGGIES

Your coals should still be burnin' hot. Lift the Dutch oven and hold your hand above the coals to see. Put another 1–2 tablespoons of oil in the pot, put the pot back on the coals, and let it heat up until the oil is shimmery again.

Once the oil's ready, toss in the onions, peppers, and garlic. They should sizzle immediately. The French word "sauté" means "jump." If the Dutch oven is hot enough, the veggies should do just that as they fall into the oil.

Stir the veggies up with the wooden spoon. Add a little salt to help draw out the moisture. Let them cook for a while, stirring occasionally. Watch and stir so that the garlic doesn't burn. Pretty soon, the onions will turn translucent. This means that the starches are turning into sugars, and the onions are going from harsh and pungent to rich and sweet. The longer you cook them, the sweeter they get. When I'm doing a chili, I usually let the onions start to caramelize a bit. You'll see them start to turn brown.

This would probably also be a good time to add a few handfuls of fresh coals to the fire, to get them ready to replenish the ones you're using under the pot.

ASSEMBLING THE CHILI

Pour in the liquid—either water, stock, or half of each, depending on what you have. I really like the richness that stock adds, so that's what I prefer. Put the meat back in and add the tomatoes. Drain any excess water off the beans and add them to the pot. Put the lid on and let it start to heat back up.

Don't put any coals on the lid. We're only using bottom heat, remember? From here on out, you'll simply maintain the coals, adding fresh ones from your fire as you go.

FLAVORINGS AND SEASONINGS

I listed some spices in the ingredients that you can start to add in. Don't be afraid of them, but it *is* possible to go overboard. This chili will be better if it cooks a long time, so you can put in some seasonings, wait 10 or 15 minutes, and then taste test.

This is particularly true of the heat. Whether you use chili powder or fresh jalapeños, take it a bit at a time. Jalapeños are pretty strong, but you can tame them quite a bit by cutting out the core and the seeds beforehand (that's where most of the heat is). In any case, dice the peppers and add them in a little at a time. Let the chili cook for a while and then check it. If it's still too tame, add more jalapeños. You can't pull spices out once they're in.

Before you use any juice from the lemons, use the paring technique to peel some of the rind off. Don't go deep into the white (called the "pith"). Later, you'll use this for more flavoring, called "zest."

Here's a trick when juicing a lemon: Hold the lemon, sliced-side up, in the palm of your off hand and, while squeezing it with your fingers, dig into the flesh of the lemon with a fork or a spoon. The juice will spill out over your hand and into the Dutch oven. Most of the seeds, however, will be caught in your hand!

SIMMERING

After the chili has had time to heat back up and it has been cooking awhile, you can see how it boils. A simmer happens when you can see boiling bubbles, but not a lot and not an aggressive rolling boil. Adjust the coals, more or less, to maintain that level of activity. Watch your coals. You may need to add more fresh ones to your fire or your chimney.

As you check the flavors and stir the chili, you might want to thicken it up some, depending on your taste. One of my favorite ways is to simply sprinkle in some corn masa, the kind used for tortillas, tamales, and corn bread. Sprinkle it loosely over the top and stir it in pretty quickly so it doesn't clump up. Just like the flavors, sprinkle some masa, let it simmer, and then sprinkle a bit more if it still needs to thicken. Putting too much in can turn your dish into a chili paste.

FINAL TOUCHES

Just before you serve the chili, mince up the lemon zest, the cilantro leaves, and the celery leaves, and stir those into the pot. The flavors of fresh herbs are strongest just as you add them in; they diminish as they cook. Garnish the bowl with a little shredded cheese, if you like, and a few smaller bits of onion you have left over . . .

CLEANUP

Since this dish has both tomatoes and chili peppers, not to mention lemon juice, there's a lot of acid here. Don't let it sit too long. Go ahead and serve it straight from the Dutch oven, but as soon as everyone has had their seconds, rinse it out. Since it's such a liquid dish, it shouldn't take any more cleanup than that.

CONGRATULATIONS! YOU'VE learned a lot about cooking in this lesson. You learned about the tools you need in your kitchen and how to use an especially important tool: your chef's knife. Take a minute to analyze and see what you've learned.

REVIEW

You learned

- what tools and equipment you need;

- about your most important tool: the chef's knife;

- how to use that knife, as well as others, in the four basic cuts: the chop, the slice, the mince, and the pare;

- about basic culinary skills, like browning, sautéing, and simmering in a Dutch oven over coals; and

- how to use your new skills to make amazing fresh chili.

ANALYSIS QUESTIONS

How did it feel using a good knife, possibly for the first time?

Was it awkward to use the knife techniques?

How did the chili taste?

How were your seasonings? Too much? Too little?

MORE SOUPS, STEWS, AND CUTS

"IT SLICES, it dices, it makes julienne fries! It chops and mixes and even has a USB port! It sings and dances and scares away zombie insurance salesmen! How much would you expect to pay for this fine kitchen accessory? But wait! There's more, more, more!"

Yes, folks, just when you thought it was safe to bust out your Dutch ovens, we're back with more. More cuts, more basic culinary stuff, and more learning how to cook in your black pot!

In many ways, this lesson is a continuation of lesson three, with a few more twists. We're going to jump straight into the recipes and, like last time, show you new cuts and techniques along the way. First will be a delicious beef stew followed by a nice, rich chicken soup with rice.

By the way, since we've already been through all those cuts and stuff, you don't have to use all fresh ingredients in these recipes. But ya can if ya wanna!

Here we go!

DUTCH OVEN BEEF STEW

TOOLS
12-inch, shallow Dutch oven

INGREDIENTS
1–2 lbs. beef or red game meat, cubed
10–12 fresh mushrooms, sliced

1 cup carrots, chopped
3 large potatoes, quartered and sliced

2–3 medium onions, sliced
2–3 cloves garlic, minced
4–5 celery stalks, chopped

2 cans (2–3 cups) beef broth
1–2 cups water, as needed

liberal drizzles of balsamic vinegar
salt
black pepper
lots of fresh, chopped parsley

2–3 Tbsp. flour
¼ cup or so water

Some other things you could add, if you wanna:
chopped green onions
1 (14.5-oz.) can diced tomatoes

THE PROCESS for this is going to be very much like the one for the chili. You'll brown the meat, sauté the veggies, then add it all together and pour on the liquids, with more flavors. It simmers for a long time to absorb all the flavors, and you add a little thickener. Finally, it's all done.

In the process, I'll show you a few more cuts, like those used in preparing mushrooms, carrots, and potatoes.

Start the whole process off by preparing all of the ingredients. Most of them you already know how to do. Here are the few that I've not talked about yet.

MUSHROOMS

When cutting mushrooms, I first rinse them off and set them aside near my cutting board. I grab one and cut off the very end of the stem, where it's the crustiest and driest. Then I set it head down, stem up on the board. Using an overhand grip, I slice it 3 or 4 times, depending on its size. Finally I toss it into its mixing bowl. Pretty simple, really.

CARROTS

Carrots could just be chopped like celery, but I like to do them thin and "on a bias." That means that they're cut at an angle instead of perpendicular, as is typical. The actual carrot pieces are bigger, but since they're still thin, they cook more quickly.

First of all, I rinse off the carrots. Peel them if you like. I don't always do that. As a kid, we used to use harsh scrub brushes to take the top layer off the carrots. That left more carrot than the peelers did. Cut off the tip and the butt end.

When I get the carrots to the cutting board, I take one and let it roll on the board for a minute until it settles. That will be the most level spot. Then I roll it back from that point 90 degrees and use the knife to shave a bit off that side.

When I put it back down, it's now much less likely to roll away. I start at the bigger end, usually. I get my hands in position for a standard chop, but I bring out my elbows so the blade is now no longer at a 90-degree angle to the carrot. It's more like a 45- to 50-degree angle, depending where you measure from.

Finally, I just start chopping as normal and put the "chips" into a bowl, ready for cooking.

POTATOES

After I rinse off the potatoes, I place one on the cutting board. I also let it roll for a minute and let it settle. Then, I use an overhand grip to slice it lengthwise in half. I flip one side down onto the cutting board and again use an overhand grip to slice it lengthwise in half.

Then, I turn it 90 degrees, get my bear claw goin' on, and chop it into ¼-inch pieces. I drop those into the bowl and then slice and chop the other half of the potato the same way. I usually put some water into the potato bowl because it's going to be a while before they're added to the stew, and contact with air will discolor the potatoes.

COOKING THE STEW

With all the food prepared, fire up the coals.

Again, you'll start off by heating the Dutch oven to build up the patina. Then heat some oil in the bottom. Once it's hot, you'll brown the meat. Pull the meat out when it's nice and seared.

Add a little more oil, heat it up, and sauté the mushrooms. How long you do it is up to you. My wife actually loves it when the mushrooms are cooked a deep brown and caramelized. You might like them fuller and fresher. Pull them out whenever they're how you like them.

Then add a little more oil and heat; sauté the onions, the garlic, and the celery. These are called the "aromatics," by the way. As you're cooking them, I'll bet you'll be able to tell why!

Once they're cooked, add in the meat, the mushrooms, and the liquid. Stir it up and put the lid on to cook. Then add in the potatoes and carrots. Replace the lid each time you add more ingredients, which will trap the heat. Usually, I'll actually just chop the potatoes and carrots at this point and add them more directly rather than keeping the potatoes in water. Once you see how much room is in the pot, add any water to bring the liquid level to where you want it.

Keep the pot simmering over fresh coals, adding in the other flavorings as you wish.

When it's close to done, mix a tablespoon or two of flour into some water and stir it up vigorously so it's runny and not clumpy. A little bit at a time, pour it into the stew while stirring. Watch it simmer and thicken before adding more so you get it to the right consistency.

Nothing beats a hot beef stew on a cold winter night . . .

. . . unless it's chicken soup with rice!

CHICKEN SOUP WITH RICE

Maurice Sendak wrote and illustrated that wonderful poem, one stanza reading:

In January
it's so nice
while slipping
on the sliding ice
to sip hot chicken soup
with rice.
Sipping once
sipping twice
sipping chicken soup
with rice.[1]

Through all twelve months he tells us of the wonders of chicken soup with rice. I'm not sure which comforts me more, the food or the memory of reading the poem with my parents.

Here you'll learn one more cool cut and a great way to thicken a soup, with a blond roux.

TOOLS
12-inch Dutch oven (Use a little more than half the ingredients for a 10-inch)
24 coals below

INGREDIENTS
1–2 lbs. chicken, cubed and uncooked, or cooked and shredded
oil

3–4 cloves garlic, minced
1–2 medium to large onions, diced
2–3 celery stalks, chopped
salt

1–3 carrots, chopped
any other veggies you want, like frozen peas or diced tomatoes
6–8 cups of water or chicken broth (or a combination thereof)
1 cup rice
juice of 1–2 lemons
salt and pepper
parsley
oregano

The Roux

TOOLS
8-inch Dutch oven
10 coals below

INGREDIENTS
2–3 Tbsp. butter
2–3 Tbsp. flour

½ cup milk or half-and-half

AS ALWAYS, begin with the meat. A really great option is boneless, skinless chicken breast, thawed and patted dry. If that's what you're using, you can slice it up into 1-inch cubes, like you've done with all of the other meats.

Another option is to use shredded chicken that you cooked another day, like a roasted chicken or turkey. If you do that, then you don't have to brown the meat in the first cooking step.

You should know how to do most of the veggies by now, or at least, you can look back in the other pages and see how to do them. Even still, let's talk about dicing the onions. There are as many different ways to do this as there are chefs, and each chef seems to claim that his or her way is the best for one reason or another. I like my way, of course, even though I can't claim it. I learned it from YouTube. As I look at the other ways of dicing onions, I'm amazed at how many chefs still have ten fingers. At the very least, I think this way is safe, even if it's not necessarily the most "proper" way.

Begin by using the overhand grip to slice the onion in half, from north pole to south pole or vice versa. Then, put the onion sliced-side down on the cutting board and use a bear claw grip to slice off the stalk end. Leave the root end intact! Peel back a layer of skin but, again, keep the roots intact.

Put the onion back on the board, sliced-side down, and grip it overhand. Point the tip of the knife at the root end and cut down all the way to the cutting board, being careful not to cut the roots, as shown:

Then, cut one or two angled cuts the same way down one side of the onion, as shown:

Match those cuts down the other side. You should now have 3–5 cuts in the onion, each radiating outward from the center of the onion. The roots at the end should still *not* be cut.

Now, hold the onion in a bear claw, with the blade perpendicular to the cuts you just made, and chop the onion to the root. The onion will fall apart into tiny bits, each approximately the same size.

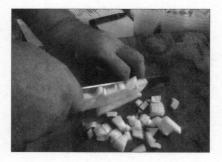

There you go! Even dices with no blood. Win!

With everything prepared, it's time to cook.

Again, get the Dutch oven hot, with a little oil in the bottom. Let it get all shimmery, but not smoky. If you're browning the chicken, toss that in first. When that's browned, pull it out.

Add a little more oil and let it get hot again. Toss in the aromatics and let them sauté. Add a little salt to draw out the moisture. This will be a light-colored soup, so I wouldn't let them caramelize.

Put the meat back in and add the stock and the other veggies. Cover it up with the lid, and check it every so often, giving it a good stir. Let it simmer to blend the flavors. Add in the seasonings and flavorings.

When it's almost time to serve it, we can thicken it up a little by making a roux.

This can be done in a smaller Dutch oven, in a cast-iron skillet, or even by turning the Dutch oven lid upside down on top of some coals.

Put the butter on and let it begin to melt. Sprinkle on the flour and begin stirring. You want it to have the consistency of a soft cookie dough. Stir and cook it for a good 10–12 minutes or more. You want it to start to smell nutty and darken a little in color. You can cook it longer and longer, until it becomes a red roux or even a brown roux. Those are often used in Cajun dishes, like jambalaya. For this soup, we want to keep it blond.

When the roux is ready, drizzle it into the soup and stir enthusiastically to make sure that it's absorbed. This alone will thicken it a little bit, but not enough. Let it simmer a few minutes more. Then gradually add the milk or half-and-half, a little at a time. The dairy will bond with the flour particles and serve to thicken the soup broth a little, making it a bit more creamy. Don't put in so much milk or half-and-half that it starts to look white, but put enough to change the texture.

Make sure to taste it and double-check your seasonings. Remember that salt can bring out the other flavors, but too much can be overpowering. Let the lemon juice carry the edge. Zest the lemons too, and mince up some fresh herbs if you want.

Finally, put the lid back on and let it simmer a bit more.

SOUPS, STEWS, and chilis are great dishes to learn cooking skills. Not only can you use lots of ingredients to enhance the basic dish, but it's also almost impossible to mess it up.

Like we do at the end of all the lessons, a bit of analysis:

REVIEW

You should be feeling pretty confident in your growing skills! In this lesson, you learned

- a few new cuts and

- some more recipes to practice your browning, sautéing, and simmering skills.

ANALYSIS QUESTIONS

How did you like your stew? Your chicken soup?

Which of all the soups and stews shown here did you like the best?

How does your knife handling feel now after a couple of dishes?

How is your overall confidence as a Dutch oven chef?

NOTE

1. Maurice Sendak, *Chicken Soup With Rice* (New York: HarperCollins, 1962), 6.

LESSON 5
HEAT AND MEAT

THE LONG, SLOW ROAST

SOMETHING THAT I discovered as I was learning to cook, which has been reinforced the more I explore it, is the universality of the processes. Think of it: there are regional cuisines and subcuisines; ovens, stoves, grills, fire pits, and solar reflectors; and all manners and ways to cook. The variation we have is simply from different options that are available to different cultures. Here's what these options all come down to:

They are all merely different ways to introduce heat to food.

I mean, when I was a kid, I took apart a toy oven. It was a light bulb in a plastic shell. But it got the air hot enough to actually bake a thin layer of cake!

It's all just heat on food. My personal choice for putting heat to my food is the Dutch oven. I enjoy grilling, and many times I cook my family's meals on my indoor stove. But still, my preference is to cook using charcoal on my Dutch ovens on the back porch.

In our previous lessons, we dealt with heat in a pretty straightforward way. I told you how many coals to use. It's time, however, for a more in-depth discussion of the nature of charcoals, heat, and how to apply that to the Dutch oven. Mastery of the Dutch oven is, really, both mastery of foods and food preparation technique, and mastery of the heat.

And here lies the real challenge of Dutch oven cooking: many more variables impact heat when cooking food outdoors as opposed to the more precise control you get on your indoor range top. When cooking indoors, you can simply turn the dial a smidge if you need just a little more or less heat. It will respond immediately and continue to put out that amount of heat pretty consistently.

To turn up the heat on a Dutch oven, you need to put in additional coals, and you need to place them as evenly as possible around the oven, and atop the oven, as needed. Then you need to give it time to raise the temperature of the cast iron and, finally, the food.

If it's cold outside or there's a breeze going, that can all change.

The bottom line is, mastering the heat of a Dutch oven requires practice. I can give you numbers and guidelines that will help you, but ultimately, you'll have to simply practice and learn. This is why I taught you to hold your hand above your coals and above your Dutch oven when you first place your coals. Do that often during cooking, and you'll learn how it should feel.

A number of popular methods are available for determining the heat needed for a Dutch oven. They vary in terms of accuracy and detail, but all are effective.

DOUBLING METHOD

This is the simplest to do, the easiest to remember, and the least precise method for determining heat. It's based on the assumption that 90 percent of all Dutch oven dishes should be cooked at an internal oven temperature of about 350 degrees Fahrenheit. It's also based on the assumption that 90 percent of all Dutch oven dishes require more topside than bottomside heat. To get to this temperature, begin with the diameter of the Dutch oven lid, in inches. Double that number, and that's the approximate number of coals you should use to get 350 degrees. Then put about ⅓ of that total under the Dutch oven and ⅔ of it on the lid, and that will give you 350 degrees once the oven heats up.

For example, I have a 12-inch, shallow Dutch oven. If I were to follow the formula, my equations would be

$$12 \times 2 = 24 \text{ total coals}$$

$$24 \div 3 = 8 \text{ coals below}$$

$$24 \text{ (first equation's total)} - 8 \text{ (second total)} = 16 \text{ coals above.}$$

If it's a deep Dutch oven, or if it's cold outside, add 3–4 coals to the total, then divide it out. Other variables might come into play as well.

Actually, I recommend using a few more coals, especially when you're starting a dish, just to heat it up quicker, even in the summer.

COAL-COUNTING METHOD

You can find charts and tables all over the Internet for determining how many coals it takes to get specific temperatures. A while ago, I combined the information in these charts with my own experience to create this table below. I think this method is more detailed and accurate than any of the other methods outlined in this chapter, but it's also less flexible.

DO Size	300°F	325°F	350°F	375°F	400°F	425°F	450°F	475°F
8″	12–14	13–16	15–18	17–19	18–20	19–21	20–23	21–24
10″	16–18	18–21	20–23	23–25	24–26	25–28	27–30	28–32
12″	19–22	22–25	25–28	27–29	28–32	30–33	33–36	36–40
14″	24–28	27–31	30–33	32–35	35–38	38–41	40–43	43–47

To use the table, simply cross-reference the size of the Dutch oven with the heat required. That will give you the number of total coals to use. (Use higher numbers if it's a cold, wintry day and lower numbers in the heat of summer.) Then you can split it 33/66 or 50/50, for the top and bottom, depending on the cooking style you're using at the moment. This is a good reference number, but I don't hold fast to it. Also, I tend to start with a few extra coals anyway.

RING METHOD

Another simple method of setting out the coals is gaining a lot of popularity. Rather than counting out the coals, you simply create rings of coals. To make a ring, form a circle with your coals so that each coal is close to its neighbor, even touching. A half ring would be set up the same way, but be missing every other coal.

Smaller Dutch ovens will, by their very nature, have smaller rings. Larger briquettes will result in fewer coals in the rings, but their size will compensate.

This system is also less detailed and precise than the coal-counting method, breaking the cooking process down into four basic heat measurements: slow (up to about 300°F), medium (350°F), hot (400°F), and very hot (450°F). In most cases, I've found that you don't need to be any more precise than that, even in baking.

DO Size	Slow	Medium	Hot	Very Hot
8"	½ ring	¾ ring	1¼ rings	1½ rings
10"	¾ ring	1 ring	1½ rings	2 rings
12"	1 ring	1½ rings	2 rings	2½ rings
14"	1½ rings	2 rings	2½ rings	3 rings
16"	2 rings	2½ rings	3 rings	3½ rings

The rings in the chart are the amounts for the coals you put above the lid. In all cases, put one ring on the bottom. In long cook times as coals burn down, fill in the empty spaces with new coals.

In all cases, no matter which method you use, when you first set your coals, hold your hand about a foot above the cooking surface, and then again above the Dutch oven, to get a good feel for the heat rising off the coals. Learn to feel the heat. Be one with the charcoal, grasshopper . . .

KINDS OF COOKING AND COAL PLACEMENT

Not only will the size of the Dutch oven, the target temperature, and the weather make a difference, but the cooking method you're using on a particular dish will also have a big impact on your coals and how you place them.

The four basic cooking methods you'll use in Dutch oven cooking are baking, roasting, sautéing, and simmering. There are others, and their names will be a bit misleading as well. For example, you'll often use the baking technique for things that aren't really about baking. That method is the most common, so we'll talk about it first.

Baking

In the baking method of Dutch oven cooking, you'll have more heat on the top and less on the bottom. Typically this will mean ⅔ of the coals above and ⅓ of the coals below. This is so that the air inside the Dutch oven gets heated and the food is less likely to burn on the bottom. The coals on the lid keep much of the heat from rising off the top. Around 90 percent of everything I cook—even though it's not really a "baking" kind of dish—is done this way.

In this method, I place the coals in rings, even if I'm not really using the "ring" method to determine how many coals to use. The underside coals should be just underneath the edge of the Dutch oven so the rising heat from the coals heats the bottom and radiates up the sides. The heat will then spread toward the center. Too many coals in the center can create hot spots. On top, the coals are also placed in a circle, just inside the rim. Extra coals can be placed in a second circle.

Roasting

The roasting method is for when you want a little more heat on the bottom, with some heat on top. A fifty-fifty split of coals, top to bottom, is how you set up this cooking method. It's great for meats and long cook times because there's usually some liquid on the bottom to help distribute the heat, so you don't have to worry as much about the food on the bottom burning. As with the baking method, I also position the coals in rings.

Sautéing

Sautéing is a bottom-heat-only method. You simply put a lot of coals underneath the Dutch oven and get the pot very hot. We talked about this in the last two lessons. I've also used this method when pan-searing steaks or cooking fish or chicken as I would on a griddle or skillet. Usually, when I'm using this method, I have the lid off.

When using the sauté method, placing the coals in a single ring under the outer edge of the Dutch oven doesn't work. Since there are a lot of coals and you're only doing bottom heat, you have to put them all underneath. One way to do that is to create several rings, one at the outer edge and others farther in. Or you can simply scatter the coals so they're spaced evenly. I leave an open space in the middle for better air circulation. I've seen coals in the center of a bunch actually go out because the outer coals were using all of the oxygen!

The Dutch oven will get very hot, and there will be hot spots as well. In most cases, you're stirring up the food, or you're dealing with liquids, so hot spots aren't as big of a deal.

Simmering

Simmering is just like sautéing, except that you have fewer coals because it isn't as hot, and you usually have the lid on. Even still, there probably won't be any coals on the lid while you're simmering a stew.

REPLENISHING AND MANAGING YOUR
HEAT DURING LONG COOK TIMES

In our last two lessons, we talked about adding coals to the simmering stew or chili to keep the heat on. This is an important part of Dutch oven cooking, and it's what this lesson's prime recipe will teach. You should keep the heat fairly steady over a long period. To do that, keep a side fire going, constantly refreshing it with unlit coals so you can maintain a supply to add to the burnouts on the oven.

I've found that the metal-cylinder chimneys are great for these side fires.

It's also useful to have a natural-bristle hand brush to whisk off the ash shed by the coals. The ash insulates and can keep the full heat from reaching the Dutch oven and, ultimately, the food. Plastic-bristle whisk brooms don't work: the bristles will melt and curl on contact with the hot oven lid.

To get some practice doing long cooking times, you can't get much better than a roast. Here are a few of my best roast recipes. I'm going to talk you through the first one, which is a perfect lesson in heat management. Its delicious meat and fall-apart texture is all due to its long, slow, low-heat roasting time.

Before we go any further, as you look over the recipe, I hope you'll notice that I recommend a deep Dutch oven. These are a lot like the basic 12-inch that you've already got, but another two to three inches deeper. I've done roasts (particularly smaller ones, like 3 pounds) in the shallow Dutch ovens, but for the larger roasts, I recommend the deeper oven. In addition, it will work better when you cook the chicken in the next lesson.

Trust me. Go buy one. You won't regret it.

If you can't get one, you can still forge ahead!

TOMATO AND VEGGIE ROAST BEEF

TOOLS
12-inch, deep Dutch oven
8–10 coals below
10–12 coals above

INGREDIENTS
3- to 5-lb. beef roast
3–4 garlic cloves, minced
liberal shakes of kosher salt
liberal shakes of coarse ground pepper
about 1 Tbsp. olive oil
not-so-liberal shakes of cayenne pepper

3–4 large potatoes
3–4 medium onions
1–2 fresh tomatoes, diced
2–3 celery stalks, sliced
fresh parsley, minced

START BY thawing the roast. Put it in the fridge for a day or two, then put it in the sink with some cool water. A hint: take it out of the package and off of the

Styrofoam tray, then put it in a zip-top bag before putting it in the water. The Styrofoam tray will insulate the meat and make it take longer to thaw.

Once it's thawed, mince the garlic. Rub it, along with the salt and pepper, onto the meat. Let it sit by itself for a while.

Next, light up some coals. When they're white on the edges, put 18–22 coals on your cooking space in a couple of rings, making sure to leave a few coals burning in the pile or the chimney. Put the Dutch oven on the coals and pour in about a tablespoon of olive oil. Let that preheat. Once the oil looks "shimmery," put the meat on. It should be so hot that it sizzles immediately. Let it sear and brown on each side for a few minutes.

Once the meat is browned on all sides, with a good caramelized sear, set it flat in the middle of the Dutch oven. Pull the oven off the coals and put on the lid. Arrange the coals, in the amounts shown above, in a circle on the cooking space and on the lid. Set the Dutch oven back on the coals. When you hold your hand above the coals for this dish, the air won't be as hot as it has been for the other dishes you've cooked so far.

At this point, 20–30 minutes have probably passed since you first set the coals out to heat the Dutch oven. By now the coals will be starting to burn down. Pour some fresh ones, maybe a dozen or so, into the fire. Mix them up, so they'll all get lit evenly.

Now you can start cutting up the vegetables. I cut the potatoes into quarters, mostly using the overhand cuts, and then cut them into ¾-inch blocks. Peel and quarter the onions. Keep these separate from the other veggies.

Once the veggies are ready, lift out the roast and put in the onions and potatoes. Stir them so they create a layer on the bottom. Put the roast back in, on top of the layer. Finally, scatter the celery and the carrots to fill in the gaps alongside the meat. If you're using a 12-inch, shallow Dutch oven, leave the meat on the bottom of the oven and pour in as many of the veggies as you can around the sides.

Close the lid and put on some fresh coals. Also, use your coal tongs to knock the ash off the older coals. The idea is to cook it at 200–250 degrees for 4–5 hours.

From this point on, it's just a matter of keeping the heat steady with fresh coals. About every 20–30 minutes, depending on the breeze, put 3–4 new coals above and 3–4 new coals below the oven. Add more coals from your bag to the side fire and mix them in.

After a while, there will be a lot of ash on the lid and under the oven. This will need to be removed because it will actually insulate the oven and protect it from the heat. Just in case you're wondering, that's *not* what we want!

Here's how I deal with it:

I use the tongs to pile up all of the coals, large or small, on one side of the lid. I shake the ash dust off as I go. Soon, all of the coals are on that side. I take my natural-reed whisk broom and brush off the ash, cleaning that half completely off. Then, I move all the coals back to the first side, still shaking off the ash as I go. I brush off the remaining ash. Be careful, by the way, because the dust is hot. Finally, I redistribute the now-clean coals over the now-clean lid. You'll be surprised how much heat you'll feel coming off the lid. As a final touch, I add more from the fire if I need to.

Then I lift the Dutch oven off the coals and do the same thing to the bottom layer.

Normally when cooking meat, you'll want to keep a thermometer in it. In this case, it will pass the "well-done" point about midway through the cooking. We want to cook it until it starts to fall apart. As you're getting to what you think is the end, grab a couple of forks and try pulling the meat apart. It should offer no resistance.

During the last hour to hour and a half of the cooking, I'll open the oven about every 20 minutes or so and spread some of the veggies and juices over the roast.

When it's all done and ready to serve, bring the roast to the table and let it sit, covered, for 10–15 minutes. In our house, this is usually how much time it takes to get everyone to the table, anyway. Serve it sliced with the potatoes and other veggies on the side. I love the blend of the seasonings with the tang of the tomato.

You could, if you wanted to, use a basting syringe to pull some of the juices from the bottom of the Dutch oven and make a gravy with cornstarch or flour. But that would require yet another Dutch oven, an 8-inch, and you wouldn't want to go out and buy another Dutch oven, would you?

Would you? No, of course not . . .

WHAT YOU just read, and hopefully cooked, is a fairly straightforward roast recipe. If you want to get a bit fancy, you can try this next one, which adds an extra ingredient—the bacon—and an extra step—the glaze. The final flavors are inspiring. Really, with the pull-apart meat, it's incredible edibles!

DUTCH OVEN ROAST BEEF WITH BALSAMIC GLAZE

TOOLS
12-inch, deep Dutch oven
8–10 coals below
10–12 coals above

INGREDIENTS
2 Tbsp. olive oil
3–4 cloves garlic, minced
kosher salt
coarse ground pepper
3- to 5-lb. beef roast

3–4 large potatoes
3–4 medium onions
1–2 carrots, sliced
2–3 celery stalks, sliced

½ lb. bacon

½ Tbsp. coarse ground pepper
1 Tbsp. kosher salt
1 Tbsp. olive oil
3 Tbsp. balsamic vinegar
½ cup honey, maybe a little more

THE PROCESS for this recipe is pretty much the same as the previous method, except for these changes:

- When you put in the veggies, peel off the bacon strips and drape them over the meat. I usually use thick-cut, peppered bacon, and I usually cut the strips in half. During cooking, the fats of the bacon will render out and make the meat that much juicier and more flavorful.

- When the roast is happily cooking, we're going to kick it up a notch. About 1 hour before serving time, make the honey and balsamic vinegar glaze: Mix all of the final set of ingredients together and dab it over the meat with a basting brush. It will seep down between the bacon slices and soak into the roast. You probably won't use all of the glaze at once, but after another 15–20 minutes, you can add more to the roast.

The balsamic vinegar, the sweet and sour of the honey, and the saltiness of the bacon all add a delicious "overtaste" to the meat. It's *amayyyzing*!

A MEDIUM–COOKED, SLOW ROAST BEEF

AS AN alternative to the long, slow overcook of the previous recipes, here's another approach. This is still a slow, low-temperature cook, but instead of roasting it for many hours until it's fall-apart soft, you roast it a few hours to a nice, soft, juicy, medium, pink-in-the-middle doneness.

This requires a bit of timing. The process is similar to those in the previous two recipes. You still sear the meat and put it on with the same amount of coals. You still put in the veggies and the bacon. The difference is that at the same time, you also put in a thermometer. Use one of those that can withstand heat, so you can leave it in the roast with the lid on the Dutch oven.

As you cook, watch the internal temperature of the meat carefully. I anticipate only a 2–3 hour cook time, depending on the weight of your roast and how well the heat is maintained.

Once the temperature is at about 140 degrees, or maybe 135, take the oven off the coals. This is usually where "rare" is. Set the meat aside in the Dutch oven, covered, while everyone gathers to the table. In about 15 minutes or so, the residual heat in the meat and the cast iron will raise the meat's temperature to about 145 degrees, a perfect medium. Slice it up and serve it with your veggies!

The process you choose depends on how you like your meat. Personally, I love it both ways.

CONGRATULATIONS! YOU'VE just cooked a delicious, slow-roasted pot roast worthy of a memorable family Sunday dinner or maybe to be served up to some friends. Maybe you even cooked a couple different roasts. Look how far you've come! Take a breath and analyze what you've learned.

REVIEW

You learned

- how to utilize charcoal briquettes to heat your Dutch oven;

- different methods for using the right amount of coals;

- how to manage coals to maintain a consistent temperature over a long cook time; and

- three great ways to cook a delicious black-pot roast.

ANALYSIS QUESTIONS

How did your roast taste?

Did you like the doneness? The texture?

What would you do differently next time?

HERBS, SPICES, AND FLAVORINGS

HERB—ROASTED CHICKEN

IF YOU'RE anything like I was, you've probably got a spice rack, drawer, or cabinet that's cluttered with little cans, jars, and baggies that have been sitting unused for years. You might have even inherited some of them from when your grandma died.

Lemme tell ya. Spices and herbs aren't like cheese or Bugs Bunny cartoons. They don't get better with age.

It's time to tackle all of that clutter and freshen up. I would recommend you throw it all away and start over. That's not always easy to do, though, and I understand that. Spices can be expensive. Plus, your situation can be overwhelming. Which spices do you really need? Which ones should you buy? Should you buy them whole and grind them yourself? What to do, what to do?

Well, in this lesson we're going to tackle flavorings in a big way. I've learned to not be afraid of seasonings. These will give life to your dishes. I have to confess that sometimes I'm eating at a friend's home, or even at a restaurant, and the dish is just bland. I would never say anything to them, but the thought crosses my mind, "If only there were a shake of this or a sprinkle of that, this dish would have leapt off the plate!"

A BIT OF HISTORY

Spices and other flavorings have been in use almost since there have been people eating. In the Middle Ages, spices also helped to preserve food, as many of them had antiseptic properties, slowing the growth of bacteria. As Europeans traveled and traded cross-culturally, particularly in the Middle and Far East, spices came to drive the world's economy. From the eighth century well into the fifteenth century, Venice and other Italian city-states became rich through their monopoly of the Middle Eastern spice trade. Much of the later flowering of art and culture known as the Renaissance was fueled by that accumulated wealth.

In the meantime, explorers like Portugal's da Gama and Spain's Columbus—funded by royalty and investors looking to break the Italian monopolies—found new trade routes to India and discovered the New World. The latter brought new flavors to the table: allspice, chili peppers, vanilla, and chocolate.

Fleets were launched and wars were fought over the spice trade. Pretty amazing to think of that much history behind all the clutter in your cabinet, right?

WHAT DOES IT ALL MEAN?

None of this, however, helps me to understand. I've spent a lot of time trying to figure out the answer to this question: What spice should I use in this dish?

I haven't found a lot of answers. Some guidelines exist, like categorized lists of herbs and spices with suggested applications. These are useful, and I relied on them for a long time. I still didn't *get* it, though. I was just following traditions and formulas. I felt as if, as long as I didn't understand spices, I would be forever locked in a world of following other people's recipes, and I wouldn't be able to explore on my own.

I tried to break out of the traditional formulas. I went through my phases. I would experiment with a certain spice and use it over and over in different situations. My family still teases me about my "cinnamon phase," and I'm still in the middle of lemons.

THE LEAP OF FAITH

Let's go back to your spice cabinet. See, commercially ground spices, like those in the little bottles you see, have a flavorful shelf life that's actually measured in months, not years. The oils that hold the flavor dissipate in the air. If a spice is ground, it will have more contact with the air, so it won't last as long. As a result, it's probably time to clean them out and get some fresh ones so you'll actually have some flavorful flavors. If you're really daring, you can throw them all out at once, or you could replace a few each paycheck. I actually recommend getting the smaller half-bottles. You'll naturally run out more often, so you'll replace them more often, keeping them more fresh. Mark the date on the labels so you can start to track them.

SPICES

Here are the twenty herbs and spices that I recommend you stock (twenty, that is, not counting the obvious two). This list is, by no means, comprehensive. You will need many, many more. I just find that I don't use them as much.

THE OBVIOUS TWO

Salt: Duh. Salt brings out everything else's flavors. For some reason, I like coarser grains of salt, like ground or kosher salts. Sea salts can be quite flavorful too. But the ordinary stuff on the table is great. Be bold, but with a little caution. Too much salt ruins the dish.

Black pepper: Another flavor that I think is underused. My mother-in-law knew how to use pepper. I like it coarse ground.

HERBS

Basil: Useful in Italian dishes.

Oregano: Great for Italian, but Mexican cuisine uses this a lot as well.

Rosemary: Wonderful for soups, meats, and rustic breads.

Cilantro: Mexican and other Caribbean cuisines rely on cilantro. I keep some dried, crushed cilantro in the cabinet, but I also use it fresh a lot.

Parsley: Like cilantro, I also use this fresh a lot, especially for chicken and veggies. I like the flat-leaved Italian parsley better than the curly leaf that's usually used as a garnish.

Mint: I love fresh mint on desserts, but you'd be amazed what it adds to a meat dish. Like cilantro and parsley, I use mint both dried and fresh.

Sage: Great on chicken.

Thyme: I'll skip the obvious joke about saving it in a bottle . . . But I'll tell you that I use it a lot in soups, stews, and meats like fish or chicken.

SPICES FOR SAVORY

Cumin: Used a lot in Mexican dishes

Curry powder: Usually I don't like to use commercial blends. I like to make my own. But a good, basic curry powder is very useful.

Garlic powder: I usually use freshly minced garlic. Occasionally, that's not practical, so garlic powder works well. I don't use garlic salt. I'd rather add in the salt I want and the garlic I want and not be locked into their predetermined proportions.

Paprika: A key part of my own homemade seasoned salt. Most of my meat rubs start with salt, pepper, and paprika.

Chili powder or cayenne pepper: For when you want to kick it up. Just a little will make a dish go from flat to vibrant. A little more will give it some actual kick. Obviously, Mexican and American Southwest meals use these hot flavors, but so do Cajun and even many Asian dishes.

SPICES FOR SWEET
Cinnamon: In my experimentation, I was surprised where this one could go. It's not just for dessert anymore. I like it in my pancakes and even in sauces and chili.

Nutmeg: This is cinnamon's not-so-pretty sister, but they work well together.

Cloves (whole and ground): Traditionally a big part of a ham, because hams are the perfect blend of savory and sweet.

Powdered ginger: Asian dishes use a lot of ginger, but mostly fresh. A lot of English and American desserts use it powdered.

LIQUIDS
Vanilla: Such a ubiquitous flavoring. Cookies, drinks, cakes, everything!

Lemon juice: This raises the zing without all the sodium that salt has. A soup or a chili just pops with lemon juice!

Honey: It's sweet and natural. What's wrong with that?

AN EXPERIMENT

In my effort to learn about various flavorings, I felt a need to really learn what they taste like. I wanted to taste them uniquely, individually, and clearly. I decided to try a tasting experiment.

EQUIPMENT AND INGREDIENTS
tiny ingredient bowls, or a small dish
unsalted butter
various spices and herbs
a butter knife
a long loaf of French bread from the supermarket
a computer, or a notebook and pencil

INTO EACH ingredient dish, I put a tablespoon of butter (I let it soften at room temperature first). I did five spices at a time, mainly because that's how many little dishes I could find. Into each dish, I put a half teaspoonful of a different spice. I used the butter knife to mix it thoroughly. I let the dishes sit for about 15 minutes.

I chose French bread and unsalted butter because I wanted to taste the flavors of the spices and the herbs against something as neutral and common as possible. French bread has no enrichments like eggs or sugar. Unsalted butter is, well, un-salted. I let it sit because many spice flavors are carried and even activated by oils, so I figured the butter would enhance it.

Then, one at a time, I spread some of the butter on the bread and tasted it. Next I took notes describing the flavors. One thing I learned was just how inadequate words are in describing taste. Even still, the notes helped me to remember the distinct flavors. Many tasted just as I expected them to, like garlic. Others, like thyme, completely surprised me.

Then I took a break, cleaned out the dishes, grabbed five more spices, and followed the process again.

I tell you, if you do this experiment and then do it again a week or two later, you'll find yourself understanding your flavorings much, much better.

Here are some of the spices I tasted and my thoughts as I tried to write down the flavors:

- Allspice was very bitter with a bit of a sting. Almost cinnamony and kinda smoky too.

- Ground cloves were tart and spicy, even zingy. The flavor was strong and dominated my mouth for a while. I had to eat some unflavored bread and butter to get the taste cleaned out for the next tasting.

- Ginger was edgy, almost hot. I wasn't really surprised by the flavor, since I'd had gingerbread and ginger candies before. Still, I was surprised by the strength. It also had a residual taste.

- Cumin has a sharp tang to it. It's like a number of flavorings with a sort of woody taste that follows the sharpness.

- Dill was a surprise. I thought I knew dill, because I'd eaten pickles. But much of that flavor is made by the vinegar. The herb itself is sweet, with a bit of zing.

- Parsley also surprised me. There's a bit of bitterness and a deeper taste that comes on late. It's kind of . . . I dunno . . . "grassy"?

- Paprika tastes just like what it is: a smoky or charred sweet pepper. The smokiness gives it a little bitter edge, but not distastefully so.

- Nutmeg is also bitter, smoky, and woody. This was one that I had whole, so I grated it with a zester into the butter. It surprised me that it goes so well in sweet and rich foods like pies and creams, because it's not sweet or rich itself.

- Garlic powder was exactly what I thought garlic should taste like. It's kind of unmistakable. It's tangy, savory, sparky, strong.

- Thyme was a big surprise and very hard to describe. It "lightened" up my mouth and left it feeling broader. It was the opposite of puckering or tightening.

- Cinnamon is so common I knew what it would taste like, but I wasn't ready to taste the zesty heat without the usual accompanying sweetness that something sugary normally gives it. The edge is somehow edgier that way.

I think the very act of tasting them and forcing myself to try to describe them has created a sensory memory for me and has made me better able to think of how I can utilize these flavors. I strongly recommend you try this experiment.

I mean, really, try it. This weekend! It will do wonders for your cooking!

SOME COOKIN'

Okay, now that we've talked about spice history and theory a lot, it's time to get cooking.

I mentioned earlier that I don't like to buy spice blends so much. I'd rather learn what's in them and make them myself. I've included some of my favorite spice blends here along with a recipe for each one.

MARK'S SEASONED SALT

Seasoned salt is a common mix. A long time ago, I looked online for recipes and found a lot of variations. Some were complex, others simple. But in the end, I morphed what I saw into this one. I really like it, merely for good taste. To make it into a basic meat rub, sprinkle on liberal amounts of coarse ground black pepper.

3 Tbsp. salt
¾ tsp. paprika
½ tsp. onion powder
½ tsp. garlic powder

Here's one easy way to use it for a tasty side dish:

MARK'S SEASONED ROASTED POTATOES

TOOLS
12-inch, shallow Dutch oven
12–14 coals below
13–15 coals above

INGREDIENTS
vegetable oil
3–4 large potatoes, quartered and sliced to ¼ inch
2 medium onions, diced (optional)
2 Tbsp. olive oil
liberal shakes of Mark's Seasoned Salt
liberal shakes of coarse ground black pepper

LIGHT UP the coals and, when the edges are white, put them all on the cooking surface. Put the Dutch oven on the coals with a thin spray or wipe of vegetable oil. Let it heat the oven and enhance the patina. While the oven is heating, slice and chop up the potatoes and onions, if desired.

Drizzle in the olive oil and let it heat until it's shimmery. Then pour in the potatoes and onions, stirring them all around to get a good oil coating on them. While you're stirring, sprinkle on the spices. Let the veggies get good and coated. Finally, put the lid on the Dutch oven and set the coals above and below. Roast the potatoes for about 30 minutes or so. Taste one to see if it's as tender as you like it and if the seasonings are right. This would make a great side dish for a soup or a meat.

MARK'S BLACKENING MIX

One of my favorite lines seen on an apron: "It's not burned, it's Cajun!"

I *love* blackened seasonings. I love it on seafood (especially salmon), chicken, even on steak. I wonder if you can blacken sandwiches. Hmmm . . . Like above, I researched a whole lotta online recipes for Cajun blackening spice mixes. This is a hybrid that I really like.

2 tsp. cumin
2 tsp. crushed coriander
2 tsp. garlic powder
2 tsp. coarse ground black pepper
2 tsp. thyme
3 tsp. paprika
3 tsp. salt
1 tsp. oregano
½ tsp. cayenne pepper

MARK'S BLACKENED CHICKEN

TOOLS
12-inch, shallow Dutch Oven
24+ coals below to start, and then
12–14 coals below
13–15 coals above

INGREDIENTS
4 boneless, skinless chicken breasts, thawed and patted dry
Mark's Blackening Mix
1–2 Tbsp. olive oil

THIS IS so simple, I'm almost embarrassed to put it into a cookbook. But it's *yummmmy.*

After the chicken breasts have been patted dry, dust them liberally with the spices, on both sides. You want the chicken dusted, but not coated. Let the chicken breasts sit for a while, covered by plastic wrap.

Meanwhile, get the charcoals lit and the Dutch oven heating up, as if for sautéing or browning. Once the Dutch oven is hot, add the oil and let that heat up as well.

Lay the chicken breasts into the Dutch oven and let them sear, uncovered, for a few minutes on each side. Then put the lid on and adjust the coals as given above. Cook the chicken for about 30 minutes, until an internal temperature check comes to 170 degrees or until the juices run clear.

Serve the breasts with rice, pasta, or potatoes, or even in sandwiches. Let them cool, slice them, and serve them in a chef salad. You have all kinds of great options!

HERBAL POULTRY SEASONING

Here's another great seasoning mix, this one more herbal, but it's for the birds. Ha! For the birds. Get it?

Okay, yeah. I'll stick with the cooking and leave the jokes to the pros.

3 Tbsp. dried, crumbled sage
1 Tbsp. dried, crumbled thyme
1 Tbsp. dried, crumbled marjoram
1 Tbsp. dried, rosemary, whole leaves
1 Tbsp. ground black pepper
1 Tbsp. celery seeds
¼ tsp. cloves, powdered

THIS CAN be used as is, or it can be powdered using a grinder or one of those small, 8-oz. cup blenders. Either way is great.

HERB—ROASTED CHICKEN

TOOLS
12-inch, deep Dutch oven
12–14 coals below
13–15 coals above

INGREDIENTS
2–3 large potatoes
2 medium onions
2 carrots
3 celery stalks

1 whole roaster chicken, thawed and patted dry
3–4 Tbsp. softened butter
Herbal Poultry Seasoning.
salt

START, AS usual, by lighting up the coals. While they're getting white edges, slice up the veggies. We're not going to preheat the Dutch oven this time.

Layer the veggies across the bottom of the Dutch oven (it's deep, remember?). Add the chicken on top, breast-side up. If this won't fit, then lighten the layer or set the chicken directly on the bottom of the Dutch oven and spread the veggies around it.

I like to poke holes in the chicken skin so the flavors soak down in. Then smear the butter all over the top of the chicken. Shake the Herbal Poultry Seasoning and the salt liberally over the buttered chicken. Close the lid and put the pot on the coals.

This is a higher-heat roast, so it'll probably be done in about an hour, maybe an hour and a half. Use a thermometer to check the breast temperature. I shoot for 180 degrees so it comes off the bones easier.

When it's done, let it rest for a few minutes in the Dutch oven, covered, before carving it and serving it with the veggies on the side.

WRAPPING IT ALL UP

Flavorings are one of the hardest things, I think, that I've had to learn in cooking. And now you've got some understanding of how they all fit together. The key is to find the balance where they're not overused but you're not timid with them either. With more and more cooking experience, you'll add more and more flavors to your palate's palette.

REVIEW

You've learned

- how different herbs and spices might be used;

- what each spice tastes like; and

- a few different spice combinations and where to use them.

ANALYSIS QUESTIONS

Were there any surprises as you tasted the individual herbs and spices?

What did your taste buds learn about flavorings?

Did you like what you cooked?

What would you do differently next time?

LESSON 7
FLOUR, SODA, AND HEAT

PART 1: BISCUITS AND SODA BREAD

THINK BACK to grade school. How many of you went through the science experiment known as the baking soda volcano? You built a large papier-mâché mountain and most likely painted it brown and green. You left a hole in the peak and placed a small cup inside. Into the cup, you poured a generous amount of baking soda. You probably set this experiment on a table in front of a trifold display showing famous volcanos and a drawing of a cross-section of a volcano.

At the moment of truth, you, the young scientist, poured some vinegar into the cup and it bubbled and boiled, pouring out and over the sides, running down the mountain, devastating the plastic village at the base.

It was a lot of fun to watch and even more fun to do. When you think about it, though, it really didn't demonstrate anything that had anything to do with volcanos.

What it did demonstrate, however, was the chemical principle of what happens when you combine an acid and a base. They react. In this case, they combine to create a lot of carbon dioxide, or CO_2.

Okay, so what does that have to do with Dutch oven cooking?

The answer: biscuits!

Well, not only biscuits but all types of breads and cakes. Without CO_2, all breads would essentially be flatbreads, like tortillas, or bricks. There would be no light and chewy breads, no puffy cakes, no flaky biscuits, and no bouncy pancakes. It's really all about another word: leavening.

Leavening is taking a mix of flour and water (among other ingredients) and infusing the dough or batter with gas bubbles. Then, when the mixture heats up, the bubbles expand, poofing out the dough until the heat cooks the ingredients, locking the structure in place.

Through the centuries, even the millennia, this has been done in several different ways. In breads, the introduction of yeast germs, fermenting, creates the CO_2. In relatively recent years (in the last two centuries) a method was developed for using chemicals to create the gas: like the volcano of your youth, an acid and a base.

The method started simply with sodium bicarbonate, or baking soda. Included with the flour and then mixed with an acidic liquid, especially a tasty one like buttermilk, the baking soda would react. The gas that the reaction produced would be caught in the flour and the fats of the buttermilk, which would leaven the bread.

This had two big advantages: One, this method could be done with softer, lower-gluten wheats, which didn't trap the yeast gasses as well. And two, the method didn't take hours or days to leaven. In fact, this process *had* to be done quickly because, if you didn't bake the mixture right away, the reaction would happen and be over before the mixture baked.

Soon, another advancement was made. The baking soda was combined with a powdered acid, like cream of tartar. The two could be kept together, and they wouldn't react until they were mixed with a liquid. Now you no longer needed buttermilk, or anything else acidic, because the base and acid combination was right there all along. This became known as baking powder.

Both of these solutions had one problem. They acted once, and when that was done, there was no more gas. Another acid was added, one that acted not when it got wet, but rather when it got hot. So the baking powder became "double-acting." It reacted when you first mixed the ingredients, and then it reacted again when it was in the oven, giving extra lift. And so the process remains to this day.

When I was young, trying to bake stuff, I wondered what the difference was between baking soda and baking powder. There you have it. Soda is a base and needs an acid to react. Baking powder, on the other hand, contains both the acid and the base and needs only water and heat to react.

In this lesson, you'll be learning how to do what are commonly called "quick breads"—namely, biscuits and a loaf of traditional Irish soda bread.

BASIC MASTER MIX

First though, we have to make the Basic Master Mix (BMM). So often, when we want to make biscuits to go along with a meal, we simply reach for the box of biscuit mix. We add in the water, and away we go. Remember, the chemicals won't begin reacting until moisture is added.

The cool thing is that this mix isn't just for biscuits. With the right additives and enrichments, you can make pancakes, muffins, waffles, dumplings, and other bread-like stuff. Just reach for the box.

Well, we like to work from scratch here, but we still like the convenience. So start off by making up your own mix. Then, when you need it, it's there, and it makes the whole experience even quicker.

5 lbs. flour (20 cups)
2½ cups powdered milk (unmixed—still a powder)
¾ cup double-acting baking powder
3 Tbsp. salt
2 Tbsp. cream of tartar
½ cup sugar
1 lb. vegetable shortening

FIRST, SIFT or whisk all of the ingredients except the shortening together. Mix it well, as the entire quantity needs to be an even balance of all the ingredients.

Then use a pastry cutter to cut in the shortening until it looks well-blended, like cornmeal. You can even use your hands to work out some of the bigger chunks and blend it all up. Once it's all mixed, store the mix in large zip-top bags or another airtight container in a cool, dry place. It keeps well for 6–8 weeks.

Here are a couple of ways to use this mix to make quick-bread biscuits.

DROP BISCUITS

I like to do drop biscuits because they're much easier than rolled. You just mix the ingredients and spoon the mixture into the Dutch oven to cook. It's ready.

TOOLS
12-inch, shallow Dutch oven
12–15 coals below
24–28 coals above

INGREDIENTS
3 cups BMM
¾–1 cup water or milk

START BY lighting up the coals and letting them get white. Then spritz the Dutch oven interior with some oil and set it on and under the coals. You'll notice that there are a *lot* of coals. The Dutch oven needs to be very hot to activate the second reaction.

Then stir up the mix and the water. You want it to be a bit sticky and gooey. Flour absorbs water differently in different circumstances, so simply add enough water or milk to make the mixture look sticky. It's not a batter, but it's not a tight ball of dough either. Stir the mixture up but don't work it. It won't be kneaded.

Open the Dutch oven and drop generous spoonfuls into it. Arrange them in the bottom and close the lid as quickly as you can, to keep it from loosing heat. Check them in 10–15 minutes. They should be fluffy and only slightly browned.

GARLIC AND CHEDDAR DROP BISCUITS

Here's a great variation to the drop biscuits above. Add these ingredients into the mix and follow the exact same procedure.

INGREDIENTS
1 cup shredded cheddar cheese
1 tsp. garlic powder
2 Tbsp. butter, melted

ROUND BISCUITS

NO MATTER what kind of biscuits I'm making, I usually follow a similar process. I start by lighting up the coals. I let them get a bit white while I gather up the ingredients and prepare my space.

When the coals are white, I put the Dutch oven (with some oil spritz) on and under the burning coals to preheat while I mix and prepare the dough. If I'm making a big batch, I might even heat up two Dutch ovens.

For the round biscuits, I start by measuring out the master mix (same amount as in the drop biscuits but with the new ingredients above) into a bowl, and then I add the liquid. I want this to be a drier dough than the drop biscuit dough. It should come together in a ball. I might use my hand a bit for the mixing, with a kind of kneading motion, but I don't do that too much. You don't want to develop any gluten, and you don't want the fats in the mix to get warm and soft; they need to trap the gas that the chemical reaction is making.

Then I dump the dough on a floured counter and flatten it out (either with a rolling pin, if I can find one, or with my hands). I flatten it to ½ to ¾ of an inch. I sprinkle on some flour and fold it over. Then I flatten it out again. I repeat this process 4–5 times, creating layers. Still, don't do this too much. The first chemical reaction has already been taking place, and you don't want to wait around too long. Here's what this will look like:

Next, I cut them into circles. I'm told that if you use a cup, don't twist it because that can let out too much gas. I've never noticed it that much. After punching out a few circles, wad the remaining dough back out, flatten it again, and cut some more. At various times, I've coated the tops with milk, butter, or beaten egg. They will give different textures and browning.

Then I take the biscuit rounds outside and put them in the ovens, which should be pretty hot by now. I put the lid on and let them start baking. I check them after about 10 minutes, at which point, if they're not done, they should be pretty close. Then I enjoy them with butter and jam, or honey!

IRISH SODA BREAD

Making a great-tasting, light loaf of "traditional" Irish soda bread has always been a challenge for me. But over time I think I've learned from my mistakes. The biggest thing for me has been to separate soda bread in my mind from yeast breads. It is a totally different animal. It tastes different, the crust and crumb are different, it lifts differently . . . It is completely different. Success or failure of a soda bread should be judged on unique standards.

A great soda bread loaf will lift up to about double its original height at the center and will split where you cut into it. This bread will have a hearty crust but will not be a brick. The crumb will be only slightly denser than a cake and will have a tangy, salty taste.

After years of attempts and failures, this recipe and this process have worked for me over and over.

TOOLS
12-inch, shallow Dutch oven
10–12 coals below
20–24 coals above

INGREDIENTS
2 cups flour
1 tsp. salt
1 slightly heaping tsp. cream of tartar
1 heaping tsp. baking soda
any enrichments (I like dried, chopped cranberries)
1 cup (½-pint carton) buttermilk

START BY lighting the coals. Once those are showing some good white burn, set the Dutch oven (spritzed with oil on the inside) on and under the coals. This will cause a lot of heat. While the oven is preheating, make the dough. This won't take long, and by the time you're done, the Dutch oven will likely be up to temperature.

Mix all the dry ingredients together in a bowl. I usually sift in the flour, mainly to aerate it, which makes the crumb a little looser. Notice, also, that I don't use bread flour. Chemical leavens like baking soda and baking powder don't rely on gluten strands to trap the gas and rise, as yeast breads do. Instead the chemicals interact, creating the gas, which is trapped by the liquid and the fats in the buttermilk. Also, the acids in the buttermilk react with the soda and produce the gas in the first place.

Make a well in the middle of all the powders, pour in the buttermilk, and gradually stir it in. Soon the mixture will clump together. Use your fingers to knead it and shape it a little bit in the bowl. This is a very important part: don't work it too much. This is *not* a yeast bread where you're kneading it for 20 minutes or more. A few squeezes and folds to mix it well and a bit of shaping and molding, and you're ready to go. The more it interacts with your hands, the warmer it gets, and you want it cold. Add in any enrichments at this point, while you're mixing.

Dump the dough out on a floured tabletop and shape it into a flat disc about 6 inches around by about 1½ inches high. This is another important part. I don't know how I missed this, but in the past, I always shaped it into a high and rounded ball. I think that had a big, big impact on how much the dough rose up and how the heat could cook into the bread. Pressing it into a flat disc gives it less bulk and the ability to rise up during baking. Shape the sides fairly smooth too.

There are all kinds of stories about why this bread is traditionally cut with a cross on top. I'm kind of a practical guy, so I know why I do it: (1) The cut allows the bread to spring up and spread. (2) It gives it a place to vent a lot of the steam as it bakes. And (3) it makes it easy to break into four even pieces once it's done.

Finally, put the dough into the Dutch oven. Stick a thermometer in the dough and close the oven up quickly! Bake it for 15–20 minutes before you check it. Make sure to rotate the Dutch oven when you check the bread. Bake it to an internal temperature of 160–180 degrees, adding coals if you need to. Resist the urge to add too many coals underneath, by the way. Watch the bottom coals and do some replenishing so they don't burn out, but don't go crazy with it. You don't want the bottom crust to be too thick.

CONGRATULATIONS! YOU'VE learned about making biscuits and other breads in a Dutch oven. These breads are a great way to enhance your meals! Not only are they delicious, but with practice they can also be impressive.

REVIEW

You've learned

- how chemical leavening works to create delicious breads;

- how to make drop and round biscuits; and

- how to make a full loaf of traditional Irish soda bread.

ANALYSIS QUESTIONS

How did the biscuits taste and did they lift?

Did your round biscuits flake into layers?

How did the soda bread turn out?

LESSON 8

FLOUR, SODA, AND HEAT

PART 2: CAKES AND SWEETS

IN THE last lesson, you learned how chemical leavens work and how to make quick breads. Now I'll teach you how to make sweet stuff! Pancakes. Cookies. Cakes. I love them all!

I found that the theory behind these foods is pretty much the same as the quick breads. I'll bet that the cakes evolved out of the breads, as people added in enriching ingredients like eggs, sugar, and other flavorings. But then, I really don't know what I'm talking about. I'm not a food historian.

Some of these will use the same Basic Master Mix from the previous chapter (on pages 98–99), and others, like the cakes, will use their own mix.

PANCAKES

TOOLS
12-inch Dutch oven lid
18–22 coals below

INGREDIENTS
3 cups BMM
1 egg
1½ cups water or milk (adjust to the consistency you like)

MAKING PANCAKES in a Dutch oven, over coals, requires that we think outside the oven a bit. While you could just cook the pancakes in the bottom of the Dutch oven, the side walls would make it difficult to get the spatula under each pancake to flip it over or to take it off when it's done.

So we turn to the lid! Dutch oven lids are clever in that they can be inverted and, with a little ingenuity, set above the coals to be used as a griddle. Lid stands are available commercially, and they're great. I especially like using them to hold the lid while I'm adding seasonings or stirring up my stew. In that case, you can use the lid stand to hold the lid above the coals.

If you don't have a lid stand, you could use three bricks or rocks or anything else inflammable that's about 2–3 inches high. You could even just rest the lid on the coals, but that would create hot spots and lessen the air circulation.

To start this breakfast, light up 20–25 coals. Keep some for your side fire. When they get white, spread 18–22 of them evenly in a circular area. Set up the lid, inverted, above the coals using the stand or whatever you've got. Make sure the lid is level or close to it. Let that preheat.

While it's preheating, mix the batter. Add all the ingredients and whisk them together. I have found that pancakes fluff more and cook better if the batter is runnier. Experiment and find the balance you like, but I like it really runny.

Spritz the underside (now facing up) of the lid with oil or spread with butter. Pour on some batter. Most Dutch oven lids will have a concave center, so the batter will flow toward the center. For this reason, do one pancake at a time. You can make them pretty big though, if you want. Camp Chef, however, makes some Dutch ovens with flat lids. Some even have legs cast into the lids.

When I do pancakes, I cook them mostly through on one side before I flip them. That means that bubbles are forming, popping, and not closing back up on the edges. Then I flip the pancake and finish it for just a few moments on the other side.

I'll usually use a plastic flipper too so that I don't scratch the black, but be careful with them, because they'll melt if you let them sit on the hot lid.

Typically, with our family, I just serve the pancakes as soon as they're done. Some-one will grab the first few, and then someone else will take the next few. If you want it to be fairer, and more like an "everyone come and sit down at the same time" kind of meal, then preheat another 12-inch Dutch oven (with another lid, preferably) with 5–6 coals below and 5–6 coals above. Put the finished pancakes into this Dutch oven to keep them warm. Make sure that it's preheated, though; otherwise the Dutch oven will draw much of the heat away from the pancakes!

Serve them how you like them! I'm a peanut butter and maple syrup kinda guy myself. Others I know like honey. Some like fruits and powdered sugar, or even whipped cream. Let your imagination run wild!

Here are some flavor variations that my family loves:

Spice Pancakes: Add liberal shakes of cinnamon and nutmeg to the mix.

Apple Pancakes: Peel and core an apple, then slice it thin and mince it up. Add this to the mix with liberal shakes of cinnamon and nutmeg.

Chocolate: Add a tablespoon of cocoa powder to the mix, and maybe even choco-late chips.

COOKIE BARS

TOOLS
12-inch, shallow Dutch oven
9–10 coals below
18–20 coals above
parchment paper

INGREDIENTS

3 cups BMM
1 cup sugar
1 egg
1 tsp. vanilla
⅓ cup water

ENHANCEMENTS

chocolate chips
nuts
raisins
oatmeal

COOKIES (AT least small, round, traditional ones) are kinda tough to do in a Dutch oven. There isn't a lot of room at the bottom, so you'd end up doing only 4 or 5 at a time. So, in this situation, we'll create a cookie-like dough; spread it around the bottom of the Dutch oven, flat; then cut it into wedges or squares when it's done and cooled.

As always, start by lighting up some coals. This time, however, we're not going to preheat the Dutch oven. We'll need that to be cool so we can spread the dough inside. Instead, we'll preheat the lid. Scatter a lot of whitening coals on top of the lid and set it aside, maybe on the lid stand.

While that's heating, mix the dough. Simply combine the ingredients and blend.

Before you put the dough into the Dutch oven, however, cut a circle of parchment paper to about the size of the bottom of the Dutch oven, and lay that in, flat. Then spread the dough on top of it.

Put the Dutch oven lid on and adjust the coals to be the correct amount (listed above), over and under. Let it bake for 10–15 minutes and check it. An easy way to tell if the dough is ready is the toothpick test: stick a toothpick in, and if it comes up clean, the dough is done!

Let it cool completely, then cut it into wedges, bars, or squares. For something more fancy, cut the cookie bars into the angled trapezoid shapes that they traditionally use for baklava. Then drizzle it with chocolate and caramel syrups!

CAKES

I love cakes! At this point in my career as a Dutch oven chef, I'm not as good at them as I'd like to be. I do okay at baking them, I'm getting better at decorating them, but I'm by far the best at eating them! Mmmmm!

Once again, to keep things simple, we're going to start our cake with a basic mix.

BASIC CAKE MIX

10 cups pastry (cake) flour
1/3 cup baking powder
8 cups sugar
1/2 cup cornstarch
1 Tbsp. salt
3 cups shortening

CAKE FLOUR is lighter and finer than all-purpose flour, and it has even fewer gluten-forming proteins. You can use all-purpose flour for this, but I've found that I like the fluffiness of my cakes better with cake flour. It's a little tricky to find in stores. I did some searching once, among the various bags of flour, and found nothing. Finally, I hid my man card and asked for help. The store employee looked with me, and together we found it packaged in a box, among the cake mixes.

Mix the dry ingredients and then cut in the shortening with a pastry-blending knife. Keep working it until the shortening is completely mixed in and it looks more like cornmeal than flour. Store it in an airtight container, like a zip-top bag, somewhere cool. Put a date on it too so that six months from now, you'll either have used it all up or you'll be ready to throw it out.

Before you start, you need to get or make some things. One is a cardboard cake round or two that are about the same size as your Dutch oven. You can buy these at any store that sells cake decorating supplies or you can make them by cutting circles out of the side of a corrugated cardboard box. The other thing you'll want to make is a circle of baking parchment paper about the same size.

Here are the cakes you can make with the mix. All of these can be baked with the same basic procedure.

DUTCH OVEN YELLOW CAKE

TOOLS
10-inch, shallow Dutch oven
6–8 coals below
12–15 coals above

INGREDIENTS
3 1/3 cups Basic Cake Mix
2 eggs
3/4 cup milk
1 tsp. vanilla
oil
flour

YOU'LL START this process just like you did the cookie bars. Light the coals, and when they get white on the edges, preheat the lid.

Then, whisk the ingredients together (except oil and flour). Oil the bottom and sides of the Dutch oven and shake a thin layer of flour over the oil, concentrating on the sides. For the bottom, put the parchment paper in place. Finally, pour in the batter.

Put the lid on the Dutch oven and then adjust the coals to be the proper amount above and below. Let the cake bake, rotating the Dutch oven after about 15 minutes. At 35–40 minutes, check it with a toothpick or a fork. If the toothpick comes out clean, it's done.

When the cake's done, take the Dutch oven off the coals. The cake and the Dutch oven need to cool for a while. I know from experience the difficulty of removing a cake from a pan when it's hot. Well, it's difficult to remove in one piece anyway.

When the cake is cool, run a knife around the edge to separate the cake from the sides of the Dutch oven. Put the cardboard round on the cake. Then while holding the round in place with one hand, turn the Dutch oven over with the other. The cake should drop out nicely. Then simply peel off the parchment. Make another cardboard round; put it in place and flip it back over.

Frost it if ya gots it.

WHITE CAKE

3⅓ cups Basic Cake Mix
3 egg whites
¾ cup milk
1 tsp. vanilla

TO MAKE the white cake, you do have to know how to separate eggs because the recipe calls for only egg whites. This can be tricky, but with practice, it's easy. In this case, separating the eggs is even easier because you're not going to whip the egg whites, so it's a little less critical if you get a little bit of yolk in with the white.

Take the egg and crack the side, just like you always do. Insert your thumbs into the crack, just like you always do.

Here's where it gets a bit different: When you separate eggs normally, you keep the egg laying sideways and pull the halves of the egg apart, dropping the whole egg into the mix. In this case, hold the egg upright over a small bowl and pull the upper half off, as if you're opening up the lid of a small jewelry box. Most of the white will drop into the bowl, and the yolk will be trapped in the lower half of the shell in your hand.

Now pass the yolk carefully back and forth from one shell half to the other, allowing little bits of white to fall into the bowl. In the end, use the white, and either discard or set aside the yolks, as the recipe requires.

CHOCOLATE CAKE

9 Tbsp. cocoa
2½ Tbsp. butter
3⅓ cups Basic Cake Mix
2 eggs
1 cup milk

IN THIS case, mix the cocoa and the butter first. Combine the remaining ingredients separately and then add the cocoa mixture to the other ingredients.

SPICE CAKE

3⅓ cups Basic Cake Mix
3 egg whites
¾ cups milk
1 tsp. vanilla
2 tsp. ground ginger
1 tsp. ground cinnamon
½ tsp. ground nutmeg
½ tsp. ground allspice
½ tsp. ground cloves

ZEBRA CAKE

THE ZEBRA Cake is one of my favorites, simply for looking amazing. You'll need two shallow Dutch Ovens of the same size (either 10- or 12-inch).

Start by lighting up enough coals to cook two cakes. When they get white, preheat the lids.

Make one batter of white cake and one of chocolate. Prepare the Dutch ovens with the oil, flour, and parchment as before. With large ladles or serving spoons, put spoonfuls of batter into each Dutch oven, alternating between white and chocolate. I put a white in each, then a chocolate in each, then a white in each, then a chocolate in each, and so on. Use different spoons for each flavor.

When all of the batter is evenly split between the two Dutch ovens, take a spoon and gently swirl it a few times through the batter in each Dutch oven. Don't mix it; just swirl it. Finally, put the Dutch ovens, lidded, out on the coals as before.

When the cakes are done and cooled, remove them from the Dutch ovens as before. Use a serrated bread knife to flatten any humps off the tops of the cake. Spread some buttercream frosting on top of one cake, and stack the other cake on it. At this point, you can decorate it as you like. Use chocolate frosting alternated with buttercream to create zebra stripes.

Or you could do the entire cake in either white or chocolate frosting and make the swirls inside a surprise.

If you've got the skills to decorate, then you can really go crazy, and people will be surprised that you made the cake in a Dutch oven!

CONGRATULATIONS! YOU can now make a great dessert or breakfast pancakes in a Dutch oven. By now, you've been through a lot, and you've learned a lot about cooking! You've come a long, long way!

REVIEW

You've learned

- how to make pancakes on an inverted Dutch oven lid and
- how to bake many different cakes.

ANALYSIS QUESTIONS

How did your pancakes turn out? Did they cook evenly? Were your coals and heat even?

How did your cakes taste?

Were you able to drop them out of the Dutch oven and decorate them?

LESSON 9
PUTTING IT ALL TOGETHER

WOW! YOU'VE come a long way; you've learned a lot.

If you started at the top of this book and did each lesson, at this point you've learned

- how to shop for a Dutch oven;

- how to make a simple dish of chicken and potatoes;

- how to clean and store your Dutch oven;

- where Dutch ovens come from and how to season them;

- what Dutch oven gear you might need;

- how to make a simple cobbler, dump cake dessert;

- how to shop for and use a good chef's knife;

- how to sauté, brown, and simmer;

- how to make great soups, stews, and chilis;

- how to measure and manage heat on a Dutch oven;

- how to handle recipes with longer cooking times, like roasts;

- how different spices and flavorings play together to make dishes come alive;

- how to roast a flavorful chicken;

- how chemical leavening works;

- how to make biscuits and soda bread;

- how to make pancakes on an inverted Dutch oven lid; and

- how to bake a cake in a Dutch oven.

You are now a Dutch oven chef! You know more than most about Dutch ovens and even about cooking in general! Remember what our goal was? It wasn't just to learn how to cook in a Dutch oven, it was to learn how to cook! And to do it in a Dutch oven.

WHAT NOW?

Let's take a chapter to put it all together. Instead of talking about one small dish or another, let's talk about cooking an entire meal in Dutch ovens. To do that, however, you might need more Dutch ovens. Let's talk about that.

DUTCH OVEN SIZE GUIDE

Size	Uses / Comments
8″	When I first got my 8-inch, I didn't think I'd use it much, but I use it a lot for rice, veggies, and other sides. I also use it often for sauces and gravies.
10″	I don't use my 10-inch much, but it really comes in handy when I'm cooking something that requires less space. Great for breads, cakes, and side dishes.
12″ shallow	This is the workhorse of my collection. I use them every week. Yes, I said "them." That means that I have more than one! You can make almost *anything* in this basic Dutch oven.
12″ deep	For those rare occasions when a whole chicken or roast won't fit in a 12-inch shallow, it's nice to have a deep oven. If you're cooking a stew or chili for lots of people, you can't beat this.
14″ shallow	I don't own one of these, and I've only encountered two or three dishes when I really wanted one. I think it would be useful when cooking main dishes for crowds.

14″ deep	I have two of these, and I use them a lot, for turkeys and hams, especially. Our family holidays would not be the same without them.
Larger	Larger sizes and shapes of Dutch ovens do exist. I've not felt a compelling urge to be found in *Guinness World Records* for owning the biggest Dutch oven of all. I would probably also be there for the man with the most pulled and/or strained muscles at a time.

Here is my recommendation for a good, basic set of Dutch ovens for family cooking:

(1) 8-inch Dutch oven
(1) 12-inch, shallow Dutch oven
(1) 12-inch, deep Dutch oven

This will allow you to cook almost anything you want. It will also facilitate cooking multiple things at once. You can use the deep 12-inch as if it were a shallow. This small collection won't cost you an arm and a leg either.

As you are able, add these to your collection:

(1) 12-inch, shallow Dutch oven (a second one for more mealtime flexibility)
(1) 14-inch, deep Dutch oven (for holiday turkeys and serving lots of people)

As you become more proficient at Dutch oven cooking, and as more of your family and friends become aware of your burgeoning skills, you may find yourself in a situation I refer to as "Mark's Black Pot, Cast Iron Rehabilitation and Acquisition Program." It's a federally nonfunded program that usually initiates when someone comes up to me and says, "I have an old Dutch oven that I never use. It's been out in my garage for years, and it's probably pure rust by now." This is the initial application for the program. It proceeds when they ask me, "Do you want it? I mean, you'd probably actually use the thing." The program engages when I say, "Sure! When can I come pick it up?"

See, I don't care how dirty or rusted a Dutch oven is. That can be fixed. It can be reseasoned.

A little under half of the pieces in my collection now are ones that have come to me through the generosity of others using this program. And the ovens they've given me have come to a good home! I use them all a lot. They are appreciated here. And I always invite the giver over for dinner a few times too, to share what I've been cooking in "his" or "her" pot!

MAKING A MEAL

So far, all we've talked about are individual dishes. That's great for learning, but one dish does not a meal make. Not usually, anyway. Typically, for a full meal, you'll want a main dish (which is usually a meat), two sides (veggies and/or fruits, and a starch or grain), and a dessert. Any of these are optional, or adaptable, of course. It's possible to make one-pot meals that have a main and side dish in one. The more dishes you have, however, the more variety there is and the more fulfilling the meal is.

CHOOSING YOUR DISHES

When I'm planning a meal, one of the most fun parts of all is going through cookbooks and finding the dishes I want to make. Start with the main dish since that will be the one you'll probably put the most effort into. Then choose compatible sides and make them easier and simpler. Then, while you're cooking the main dish, the side dishes don't overwhelm you.

PLANNING IT OUT

Every time I do a big meal, for a cook-off or for entertaining, I always plan it out. I make a chart showing each dish and when I'll want it to be done. Most of the time, you'll want everything to finish at the same time, just before serving, but some things, like breads and cakes, can be done hours before serving or even the day before.

When planning, I set up a spreadsheet. Each dish is a column, and each row is a half hour. Starting backward from the serving time, I plot out each major step of each dish. I watch to make sure that there's no half-hour slot where I'm doing too many things.

During the actual cooking, mishaps occur and things change. But with a basic plan, it's easy to adapt. You can also look ahead and figure out which of your Dutch ovens will be in use at what times; this will help you to make sure that you have enough Dutch ovens.

You should also gather the ingredients lists and make sure you have everything you'll need. Make sure you have enough coals as well. My experience has shown that you can get 4–5 complete dishes out of a single bag of coals (fewer for a long roast).

Let's say you wanted to cook a meal of the following:

Roast beef (found in lesson five on page 81)
Biscuits (found in lesson seven on pages 99–100)
Dump Cake Cobbler (found in lesson two on pages 39–40)

Here's how your spreadsheet might look:

Time	Roast	Biscuits	Cobbler
1:00	Light coals		
1:30	Brown the roast		
2:00	Begin cooking roast		
2:30		(Prepare biscuits)	
3:00		(Bake biscuits)	
3:30			
4:00	Cut veggies		
4:30	Add veggies		
5:00		Prepare biscuits	
5:30		Bake biscuits	Prepare cobbler
6:00	Serve roast	Serve biscuits	Put cobbler on coals
6:30	Dining	Dining	
7:00			Serve cobbler

In this example, there are two spots for the biscuits. One is earlier in the afternoon. If you're not feeling confident in your biscuit making, you might want to make them earlier in the day. Perhaps you only have a shallow and a deep 12-inch Dutch oven available. Then you'd have to make the biscuits earlier so you could reuse the 12-inch shallow for the cobbler. Maybe you want to take time at the very end to make some gravy in the 8-inch Dutch oven. You have many options. Planning ahead makes cooking flow more smoothly and allows you to consider these options.

After I'd been Dutch ovening for about two years, I decided that I wanted to test my skills and stretch. I wanted to plan and execute a full, seven-course meal for my family and guests, cooked entirely in Dutch ovens.

I began choosing my dishes. I tested them during my usual Sunday dinner cooking. I set a date and made my guest list. I sent out the invitations. Once I had done that, I was committed, and there was no turnin' back!

I planned and mapped out each course. Serving time would be at 7:00 p.m., and I would start cooking at 10:00 that morning. I planned my presentations to be the best plating I knew how to do at that moment. To save stress, I set up the table and the places the day before.

Finally, the day came, and I started. The time flew by, and I was having the time of my life! Only a few mishaps arose, but in the end, it was a wonderful meal. I was so proud to see my guests' reactions when I lifted the lid and started carving the roast. The day was wonderful, exhausting, and exhilarating.

COOKING FOR OTHERS

When I first got excited about Dutch oven cooking, I cooked each week. As I gained more confidence in my abilities, I wanted to share my talents with others. Believe me, as your confidence grows, so will the eagerness of your friends to receive an invitation. Cook for your family, but cook for others too. Share your newfound skills. Use this planning process to create a whole Dutch oven meal. If that's too much, do a Dutch oven main dish and cook the sides on your regular stove. It doesn't matter! Just have fun and make friends.

COOKING WITH OTHERS

There are many Dutch oven clubs and organizations all over the United States, Canada, and other countries. One of the biggest is the International Dutch Oven Society (IDOS). More information can be found at idos.org.

The IDOS is committed to preserving and promoting the art of Dutch oven cooking, and it has chapters all over the country and in many parts of the world. You can see the chapters listed on the website and find out who to contact nearest you.

The members of IDOS share Dutch oven cooking with each other primarily by these methods:

- The Cook-off. This is where Dutch oven cooks from all around get together, often in connection with some established festival, and compete to see who's the best. Most cook-offs involve three dishes: a main dish/meat, a bread, and a dessert. Winners of IDOS-sanctioned cook-offs are invited to go to the World Championship Cook-off, held each year in Utah.

- Demos. At stores or festivals, members of IDOS are often invited to help with demos, where chefs get together and cook for the public. The chefs must obey local food-handling laws, of course, and they often must acquire permits. This is a great way to share your passion with someone who may be new to Dutch oven–cooked food.

- DOGs. The Dutch Oven Gathering is my favorite event. You don't need permits, and you don't have to compete. At a gathering, you just show up and cook for each other. After everyone has cooked, everyone shares! Most chapters will host a DOG every month or two in the spring, summer, and fall—some even in the winter. I love to go to Gathering events when I can. You get to hang out with new and old friends, swap stories and ideas, and taste each other's bounteous recipes.

- The Internet. Even if you're in an area that's isolated from other Dutch oven enthusiasts, you can still enjoy the friendship of the black pot by participating in the IDOS online forums. These are found on the website, and by joining in, you can access the archives full of tips, discussions, and recipes.

FINAL THOUGHTS

Thank you for going on this journey of learning with me! Feel free to visit marksblackpot.com for more recipes and stories. Leave a comment and tell me how your big dinner went. Or tell me about a great new dish you created.

Dutch oven cooking is fun on so many levels. I've learned a life skill, and I've made strong and fast friends over my black pots. Maybe you will enjoy it too!

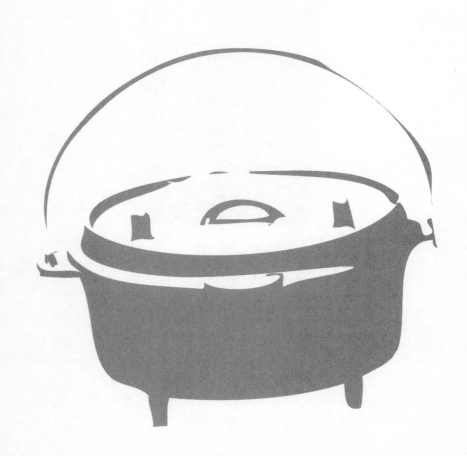

APPENDIX

MORE RECIPES

HERE, TO wrap up at the end of the book, are some more simple recipes that you can try. Many of these will help you practice the many skills and techniques taught in this book. Others are just in here because they're good!

At the end of this section, I've included a few blank forms for you to add your own recipes! Make them up or adapt them from your traditional cookbooks. When you do, you can customize them too. Then, make your own black pot blog and post it online. I'll link to you!

BASIC RICE

This side dish is essential to so many dishes. Rice is a part of virtually every national cuisine on earth. You will cook it a lot. It can be a great bed to lay just about any meat and sauce on top of. You really can't go wrong with rice, if you cook it right.

TOOLS
8- or 10-inch Dutch oven
10–12 coals below

INGREDIENTS
1 cup rice
2 cups chicken broth
juice of ½ lemon

GET THE coals ready first and then put the rice and the liquids into the Dutch oven. Really, you can use water, but I love the richness that the broth and the lemon juice add. You can also include diced veggies like peppers or celery. Do whatever will enhance the final dish that you'll be serving with the rice.

I've developed a system of cooking rice. Your own Dutch ovens may give you different results, but this never fails me. I put the filled Dutch oven on the coals, with the lid on. I don't put coals on top, I just let it heat from the bottom. In about 10–15 minutes or so, it will boil. With my 8-inch Dutch oven, I can see little plumes of steam venting out from under the lid when it's boiling. When that happens, I give it another 5–10 minutes on the coals. Then I take the Dutch oven off the coals, but I don't remove the lid. I let the rice sit, covered, for another 10–15 minutes. It can go longer, if you want. At that point it's just absorbing more liquid and cooling a bit.

Finally, right before serving, I'll stir and fluff the rice up with a fork.

RICE PUDDING

Here's an easy, creamy dessert that you can make, now that you know how to make rice!

TOOLS
10-inch, shallow Dutch oven
14–16 coals below

INGREDIENTS
3 cups cooked rice (cooked, preferably, without so much of the flavorings I suggested above)
3 cups milk (whole, preferably. I mean, c'mon, this is dessert!)
½ cup sugar
2 Tbsp. butter
1 tsp. vanilla
⅛ tsp. nutmeg
½ tsp. cinnamon
½ cup raisins

MIX THE ingredients in the Dutch oven over the coals. Stir the mixture often so it doesn't burn. Cook until mixture is creamy and hot. Then take the oven off the coals and cool it a bit. You can either serve the pudding hot, as is, or chill it for several hours (even overnight) before serving.

Here's a garnishing hint: slice some nice red apple wedges really thin, sprinkle them with cinnamon, and use them to line the edge of the bowl. Mmmmm . . .

SOUTHERN YELLOW SQUASH AND VEGGIES

When I first saw this side dish recipe, my mind went immediately to what I assumed was yellow squash. After a quick check on the web, I found out I was wrong. What I was thinking of turned out to really be butternut squash, which is hollowed out like a pumpkin or a gourd. Yellow squash is much more zucchini-like.

I suppose that you could actually use either one in this recipe, so my research really is irrelevant!

TOOLS
12-inch, shallow Dutch oven
20+ coals below

INGREDIENTS
3–4 slices bacon
1 medium to large onion
2–3 cloves garlic
1–2 small to medium yellow squash
1–2 lbs. fresh green beans
salt
pepper
paprika
parsley
juice of ½ lemon

START OFF by lighting up the coals. While they're getting hot, prepare the bacon. Slice the slices into ½-inch chunks. When the coals are hot, put them under the Dutch oven and toss in the bacon chunks. Let them frizzle (that's a technical culinary term, by the way) until they're very crispy.

Meanwhile, slice and dice the veggies: Mince the garlic, dice the onion. Slice the squash into ¼-inch slices. Snap the ends off the beans. You can snap the beans into shorter lengths if you like, or you can leave them long.

Toss the garlic and the onions into the pot and let them sauté. Add a little salt to sweat the onions some. Once the onions are translucent, stir in the other veggies and seasonings. Put on the lid, and the vegetables will naturally start steaming themselves. Don't overcook them. The beans and the squash are best when they're slightly crispy, resistant to your bite. The beans will turn a more vivid green when they're done. Serve them alongside some delectable meat that you've cooked up.

CRISPY CHICKEN CHUNKS

TOOLS
12-inch, shallow Dutch oven
10–12 coals below
16–18 coals above

INGREDIENTS
3–4 boneless, skinless chicken breasts
1 cup cracker crumbs or dried bread crumbs
½ tsp. sage
½ tsp. paprika
salt and pepper to taste
4 Tbsp. milk

FIRST, MAKE sure that the chicken breasts are fully thawed and patted dry. Then set your coals on fire.

While the coals are getting hot, slice the chicken into 1- to 1½-inch cubes. To make your cracker crumbs, choose your favorite brand or flavor of cracker and put a handful into a zip-top bag. With your fists or a rolling pin, smash them up as small as you can. Smaller tabletop or hand blenders work really well. Mix in the seasonings at the same time.

With the milk in a bowl, coat the chicken cubes. Next, shake them all up in the seasoned crumbs to get a good coating. Then arrange them in the bottom of your Dutch oven. Put the Dutch oven on and under the coals, and let the chicken bake for 20 minutes or so. Check it occasionally to make sure that the meat is well-cooked.

Serve them with ketchup or your favorite barbecue sauce, or on rice

DUTCH OVEN MEAT LOAF

TOOLS
10-inch, shallow Dutch oven
8–10 coals below
14–16 coals above

INGREDIENTS
2 lbs. ground beef or ground turkey
1 onion
1 green pepper
1 celery stalk
½ cup rolled oats
2 eggs

½ cup milk
salt
pepper

3 Tbsp. brown sugar
1 (8-oz.) can tomato sauce
parsley
oregano

ONCE YOU'VE lit your coals and they're on their way to hotness, prepare the ingredients. If you use ground beef, depending on how lean it is, you'll probably end up rendering a lot of fat and juices out of the meat by the time the cooking is done. Using turkey will do less, but then you might want to oil the side and bottom of the Dutch oven beforehand.

Dice the onion, green pepper, and celery as small as possible. Then add all of the first set of ingredients together, mix them well, and smush the mix into the bottom of the Dutch oven.

Mix the second set of ingredients and spread that over the meat mixture.

Put the Dutch oven on the coals and bake the meat loaf for about an hour. The internal temperature should be at about 160 degrees. When the meat loaf is all done, you could even sprinkle on some grated cheddar and close the lid up, letting the residual heat melt the cheese.

FLOUR TORTILLAS

Sure, you can buy 'em, but why not learn to make 'em? You'll use the "inverted lid" technique that you learned while making pancakes. The rolling or flattening technique might take a little practice, but it's not difficult. Either of the next two recipes would go great served with that from-scratch chili you made!

TOOLS
12-inch Dutch oven lid, on a stand
20+ coals below

INGREDIENTS
4 cups flour
1½ tsp. salt
½ cup shortening
1¼ cups warm water

FIRST, OF course, light the coals, and once they're getting white, set them under an inverted Dutch oven lid, set on a stand. Let the lid heat up quite a bit.

Combine the flour and the salt, then cut in the shortening with a knife, with a pastry cutter, or even by just mushing it all together with your hands. Once it's all well blended, begin adding the water as you mix and knead.

Make 16–18 dough balls by dividing the dough in half, then half again, and so on. Take each dough ball and flatten it in your hand. Then, roll it out into a 10-inch circle, maybe larger.

Place a circle right on the heated lid to cook. Soon, the dough should bubble up. When one side gets cooked and shows brown spots, flip the it over. Only flip the tortilla once. Watch and make sure that it doesn't burn. When each tortilla finishes, pull it off the lid/griddle and add it to a stack wrapped in a towel. While one tortilla is cooking, roll out another one, and keep going until you've cooked them all. Watch, because as you're cooking, you might have to replenish the coals to maintain the heat.

Finally, serve them up with chili or whatever you like.

CORN TORTILLAS

TOOLS
Dutch oven lid

INGREDIENTS
2 cups corn flour (called "masa" in the store.)
¾ tsp. salt
1+ cup water

THE PROCESS of making corn tortillas is similar to the flour variety. Start by heating up the coals and the lid, then mix the ingredients. Add the water gradually as you mix so that it's moist but still holds its shape.

Divide the dough and make 12 dough balls. Flatten one in your hand, and then flatten it more between two sheets of waxed paper, either by rolling or by pressing with a smooth-bottomed plate.

Once it's formed, put it on the lid and cook it, watching for the edges to brown. Bubbles will form, but they won't be as large as the flour tortillas had. Turn it once, then pull it off to be wrapped in a towel with the other tortillas.

ADD YOUR OWN RECIPE

NAME OF THE DISH:

CATEGORY/TYPE/TAGS:

The story behind the dish (where it came from, who thought of it):

Serves:

Size(s) of Dutch oven(s):

Coals above/below:

Ingredients (with amounts):

First Steps:

Next Steps:

End Steps, Serving:

ADD YOUR OWN RECIPE

NAME OF THE DISH:

CATEGORY/TYPE/TAGS:

The story behind the dish (where it came from, who thought of it):

Serves:

Size(s) of Dutch oven(s):

Coals above/below:

Ingredients (with amounts):

First Steps:

Next Steps:

End Steps, Serving:

ADD YOUR OWN RECIPE

NAME OF THE DISH:

CATEGORY/TYPE/TAGS:

The story behind the dish (where it came from, who thought of it):

Serves:

Size(s) of Dutch oven(s):

Coals above/below:

Ingredients (with amounts):

First Steps:

Next Steps:

End Steps, Serving:

INDEX

ABOUT THE AUTHOR

MARK STARTED cooking in his Dutch ovens in 2006, when his wife surprised him with one as a Father's Day present. His first cooking attempt was pizza, and the family instantly declared it a success! He began a tradition of cooking the family's Sunday dinners in his Dutch ovens.

In April of the following year, he thought he should start sharing what he learned, and he established the Mark's Black Pot blog. Years and hundreds of recipes later, it's still one of the most widely read Dutch oven blogs on the Internet.

Mark lives in Eagle Mountain, Utah, with his wife, Jodi, and two boys, who are also budding chefs.